Prayer Steps to Serenity

The Twelve Steps Journey
New Serenity Prayer Edition

Books by L. G. Parkhurst, Jr.

Prayer Steps to Serenity: Daily Quiet Time Edition
Abridged Edition for those not working a Twelve Steps Program
Edmond: Agion Press, 2006.

Principles of Righteousness: Finney's Lessons on Romans, Volume I
Compiled and edited from the works of Charles Finney
Edmond: Agion Press, 2006.

How God Teaches Us to Pray:
Lessons from the Lives of Francis and Edith Schaeffer
Milton Keynes, England: Nelson Word Ltd. 1993.

How to Pray in the Spirit
Compiled and edited from the works of John Bunyan
Grand Rapids: Kregel Publications, 1993, 1998.

Principles of Prayer
Compiled and edited from the works of Charles Finney
Minneapolis: Bethany House Publishers, 1980, 2001.

Answers to Prayer
Compiled and edited from the works of Charles Finney
Minneapolis: Bethany House Publishers, 1983, 2002.

Principles of Devotion
Compiled and edited from the works of Charles Finney
Minneapolis: Bethany House Publishers, 1987.

The Believer's Secret of Christian Love
Compiled and edited from Andrew Murray and Jonathan Edwards
Minneapolis: Bethany House Publishers, 1990.

The Believer's Secret of Intercession
Compiled and edited from Andrew Murray and C. H. Spurgeon
Minneapolis: Bethany House Publishers, 1988.

Prayer Steps to Serenity

The Twelve Steps Journey
New Serenity Prayer Edition

L. G. Parkhurst, Jr.

AGION PRESS
AgionPress.com

Prayer Steps to Serenity: The Twelve Steps Journey
New Serenity Prayer Edition

Copyright © 2006 Louis Gifford Parkhurst, Jr.

Published by Agion Press, P.O. Box 1052, Edmond, OK 73083-1052.

Unless otherwise noted, all Scripture quotations in this book are taken from the Holy Bible: New International Version, copyright 1973, 1978, 1984, by the International Bible Society. Used by permission of Zondervan Bible Publishers.

All Rights Reserved. No part of this book may be reproduced or transmitted in any form or by any means, graphic, electronic, or mechanical, including photocopying, recording, taping, or by any information storage retrieval system, without the prior written permission of the publisher and copyright owners.

Cover, Cover Photo, and Graphics Designs Copyright © 2004 and 2006 by Kathryn Winterscheidt. Used by Permission.

Publisher's Cataloging-in-Publication Data

Parkhurst, Louis Gifford, 1946-.

    Prayer Steps to Serenity: The Twelve Steps Journey: New Serenity Prayer Edition / L.G. Parkhurst, Jr.

    p. 23 cm.   Includes New Study Guides.

    Twelve-step programs–Religious aspects–Christianity Meditations. Compulsive behavior–Patients–Prayer-books and devotions–English. Recovering addicts–Prayer-books and devotions–English.
BV4596.T88.P37 2006   248.86 P246p
ISBN: 978-0-9778053-8-9 (pbk) New Serenity Prayer Edition
ISBN: 0-9778053-8-7 (pbk) New Serenity Prayer Edition
LCCN: 2006903856

Acknowledgments

The *New Serenity Prayer Edition* of *Prayer Steps to Serenity: The Twelve Steps Journey* contains twelve new daily meditations on The Serenity Prayer. In addition, every meditation in this new edition has been completely revised and in most cases expanded. Members of Serenity Groups (the one I attend and others) suggested some of the revisions. *Prayer Steps to Serenity* also contains many truths that I have learned while preparing and writing the weekly "Bible Lesson" for *The Oklahoman* from 1989 to the present.

A special note of thanks goes to Kathryn Winterscheidt for inspiring my visual creativity, for creating the cover and graphics designs in *Prayer Steps to Serenity*, and for creating attractive journals and gift items that encourage study and serenity in those who read this book.

I feel sincere appreciation for the late Francis Schaeffer and his wife, Edith. They became loving friends who taught me much as I studied their teachings, their commitment to prayer, and their concern for authentic fellowship. I also learned much as I wrote three of their published biographies. My emphasis on family and fellowship in *Prayer Steps to Serenity* is stronger because of their example and teaching.

As I have meditated on prayer, the truth of God, and the Bible, the writings of several other people have also deeply influenced the teachings in *Prayer Steps to Serenity*. I expanded and improved *Prayer Steps to Serenity* by using what I have learned from compiling and editing the works on prayer of John Bunyan, Charles G. Finney, Andrew Murray, the Schaeffers, Charles Spurgeon, and others. Though Andrew Murray died in 1917, the very first (and considerably smaller) edition of this book listed Andrew Murray as a co-author (because the publisher wanted to feature his name). You will find many of Murray's ideas on prayer in this book, but obviously he did not help write *Prayer Steps to Serenity*.

I owe a debt of gratitude to all those who helped me prepare the Group Study Guides for *Prayer Steps to Serenity* and the other free resources available at PrayerSteps.org, SerenityCelebration.org, CelebrateSerenity.org, and SerenityGroups.org. The help of many unnamed, but appreciated, people made a tremendous difference in my life as they have taught me, prayed for me, and helped shoulder the work that God wants done to promote His love and grace on earth. I look forward to making new friends and sharing fellowship with those practicing *Prayer Steps to Serenity* in Prayer Steps Groups and Serenity Groups, in person or online through PrayerSteps.org and SerenityGroups.org. The *New Serenity Prayer Edition* of *Prayer Steps to Serenity: The Twelve Steps Journey* and *Prayer Steps to Serenity: Daily Quiet Time Edition* (abridged for those not working a recovery program) are the result of many readers' suggestions.

The Serenity Prayer

God, grant me the Serenity
To accept the things I cannot change,
The Courage to change the things I can,
And the Wisdom to know the difference.

Contents

The Twelve Steps and Prayer—*John 14:26-27* 15

The First Step to Serenity

We admitted we were powerless to overcome our weaknesses—that our lives had become unmanageable.

Day 1   The First Step to Serenity—*Isaiah 30:18* 29

Day 2   The Source of All My Power—*John 15:5* 33

Day 3   The Good Fight of Faith—*1 Timothy 6:12* 35

Day 4   The Right Attitude in Prayer—*2 Timothy 4:7* 37

Day 5   God Meets Me in My Defects—*Ephesians 3:20, 21* 39

Day 6   God's Power Can Fill My Emptiness—*Ephesians 1:18, 19* 41

Day 7 The First Step and the Serenity Prayer—*2 Timothy 2:25, 26* 43

The Twelve Steps Journey–Step 1 Workbook—*1 Corinthians 1:25* 47

The Second Step to Serenity

Came to believe that a Power greater than ourselves could restore us to sanity.

Day 8 The Second Step to Serenity—*Hebrews 2:18* 49

Day 9 A Cure for My Anxiety—*Philippians 4:6*..................... 51

Day 10 Overcoming My Greatest Stumbling Block—*Matthew 11:28* 53

Day 11 Jesus Makes Me New—*2 Corinthians 5:17* 55

Day 12 My Power from on High—*Luke 24:49*...........................57

Day 13 The Secret of My Power in Prayer—*John 14:15-17a* 59

Day 14 The Second Step and the Serenity Prayer—*Psalm 119:66, 67*...... 61

The Twelve Steps Journey–Step 2 Workbook—*Romans 1:16a* 65

The Third Step to Serenity

Made a decision to turn our will and our lives over to the care of God.

Day 15 The Third Step to Serenity—*2 Corinthians 12:9*................. 67

Day 16 Taking Time with God—*Ecclesiastes 3:1* 69

Day 17 Willing God's Will—*Matthew 26:39* 71

Day 18 From My Strength to God's—*Psalm 84:5, 7* 73

Day 19 The Spirit Will Pray for Me—*Romans 8:26*..................... 75

Day 20 Thanking God for His Care—*Zechariah 12:10* 77

Day 21 The Third Step and the Serenity Prayer—*Proverbs 19:20, 21* 79

The Twelve Steps Journey–Step 3 Workbook—*Zephaniah 2:7* 83

The Fourth Step to Serenity

Made a searching and fearless moral inventory of ourselves.

Day 22 The Fourth Step to Serenity—*Psalm 139:3, 4* 85

Day 23 The Root Cause of My Problems—*1 John 1:8* 87

Day 24 God Reveals My Problems the Best—*1 John 1:7* 89

Day 25 The Problem of Prayerlessness—*1 Samuel 12:23* 91

Day 26 The One Who Can Save Me—*Matthew 1:21* 93

Day 27 My Reason for Rejoicing—*Luke 23:34* 95

Day 28 The Fourth Step and the Serenity Prayer—*Psalm 106:43, 44* 97

The Twelve Steps Journey–Step 4 Workbook—*Jeremiah 17:10* 101

The Fifth Step to Serenity

Admitted to God, to ourselves, and to another human being the exact nature of our wrongs.

Day 29 The Fifth Step to Serenity—*Psalm 38:18* 103

Day 30 Conscience and Confession—*1 John 1:9* 105

Day 31 Life Follows Death to Self—*John 12:24* 107

Day 32 God's Forgiveness Inspires My Love—*Exodus 34:6, 7* 109

Day 33 God Will Forgive My Prayerlessness—*Matthew 6:6* 111

Day 34 My Forgiveness Brings Singing—*Psalm 32:5* 113

Day 35 The Fifth Step and the Serenity Prayer—*Psalm 103:2-5* 115

The Twelve Steps Journey–Step 5 Workbook—*Hebrews 5:2* 119

The Sixth Step to Serenity

Were entirely ready to have God remove all these defects of character.

Day 36 The Sixth Step to Serenity—*Psalm 51:2, 3, 12* 121

Day 37 God Will Remove My Fear—*Luke 1:74, 75* 123

Day 38 Jesus Promises to Transform Me—*John 14:13* 125

Day 39 I Can Become More Like God—*Leviticus 11:44* 127

Day 40 Receiving the Fullness of God—*Philippians 2:5* 129

Day 41 Prayer Leads Me to Victory—*Romans 7:24, 25* 131

Day 42 The Sixth Step and the Serenity Prayer—*Joshua 1:9* 133

The Twelve Steps Journey–Step 6 Workbook—*Romans 5:3-5* 137

The Seventh Step to Serenity

Humbly asked Him to remove our shortcomings.

Day 43 The Seventh Step to Serenity—*Matthew 7:7, 8* 139

Day 44 God's Wonderful Promises to Me—*Hebrews 8:12* 141

Day 45 God Will Work Wonders in Me—*Ephesians 3:16, 17*..........143

Day 46 God's Love Will Remove My Hatred—*John 15:12* 145

Day 47 My Whole Life Depends on Jesus—*John 14:1* 147

Day 48 I Know God Will Help Me—*Hebrews 11:1* 149

Day 49 The Seventh Step and the Serenity Prayer— *Matthew 18:3, 4* 151

The Twelve Steps Journey–Step 7 Workbook—*James 1:21* 155

The Eighth Step to Serenity

Made a list of all persons we had harmed, and became willing to make amends to them all.

Day 50 The Eighth Step to Serenity—*Luke 19:8, 9* 157

Day 51 Some Benefits of Making Amends—*John 13:34*................159

Day 52 Forgiving Helps Me Make Amends—*Mark 11:25*..............161

Day 53 I Will Take Up My Cross—*Matthew 10:38, 39* 163

Day 54 Willing to Give Up Everything—*Luke 14:33* 165

Day 55 Willing to Face What I Lack—*Mark 10:21*.....................167

Day 56 The Eighth Step and the Serenity Prayer—*1 Peter 3:8-12*........169

The Twelve Steps Journey–Step 8 Workbook—*Proverbs 14:9*............173

The Ninth Step to Serenity

Made direct amends to such people wherever possible, except when to do so would injure them or others.

Day 57 The Ninth Step to Serenity—*Philemon 1:18, 19* 175

Day 58 I Will Avoid Making Excuses—*Philippians 2:14, 15* 177

Day 59 The Holy Spirit Will Help Me—*John 16:14* 179

Day 60 When Christ Is My Life—*Colossians 3:4* 181

Day 61 Prayer Helps in Making Amends—*Ephesians 6:18* 183

Day 62 I Will Not Give Up—*Luke 18:1* 185

Day 63 The Ninth Step and the Serenity Prayer—*Romans 12:17, 18* 187

The Twelve Steps Journey–Step 9 Workbook—*1 Corinthians 13:5-8* 191

The Tenth Step to Serenity

Continued to take personal inventory and when we were wrong promptly admitted it.

Day 64 The Tenth Step to Serenity—*Psalm 139:23, 24* 193

Day 65 Reasons for Lack of Prayer—*Romans 12:3* 195

Day 66 Overcoming Satan—*Ephesians 6:12* 197

Day 67 I Train with a Goal—*1 Corinthians 9:26, 27* 199

Day 68 Abiding in Christ—*2 Corinthians 4:10, 12* 201

Day 69 I Died on Christ's Cross—*1 Peter 2:24* 203

Day 70 The Tenth Step and the Serenity Prayer—*Colossians 1:9-12* 205

The Twelve Steps Journey–Step 10 Workbook—*Proverbs 28:13* 209

The Eleventh Step to Serenity

Sought through prayer and meditation to improve our conscious contact with God, praying only for knowledge of His will for us and the power to carry that out.

Day 71 The Eleventh Step to Serenity—*1 Timothy 4:8* 211

Day 72 True Prayer Leads to True Fellowship—*Colossians 1:27* 213

Day 73 God Will Not Forsake Me—*Psalm 9:10* 215

Day 74 I Am Crucified to Overcome—*Galatians 2:20* 217

Day 75 Reasons for Effective Prayer—*James 5:16* 219

Day 76 Reasons for Daily Prayer—*Luke 11:3* 221

Day 77 The Eleventh Step and the Serenity Prayer—*Revelation 7:11, 12* .. 223

The Twelve Steps Journey–Step 11 Workbook—*2 Corinthians 13:4* 227

The Twelfth Step to Serenity

Having had a spiritual awakening as the result of these steps, we tried to carry this message to others, and to practice these principles in all our affairs.

Day 78 The Twelfth Step to Serenity—*Mark 16:15* 229

Day 79 The Power of Intercession—*2 Corinthians 5:20* 231

Day 80 God Calls Me to Tell Others—*Acts 1:8* 233

Day 81 What May Set Me Apart—*John 15:26, 27* 235

Day 82 My Personal Testimony—*Acts 4:31, 32* 237

Day 83 My Future Work: Carrying the Message—*Matthew 4:9* 239

Day 84 The Twelfth Step and the Serenity Prayer—*Ephesians 1:3*........ 241

The Twelve Steps Journey–Step 12 Workbook—*Galatians 6:2*........... 245

Rejoicing in The Twelve Steps Journey—*Philippians 4:4-7*............... 247

Creating Your Own *Serenity Journal*.................................... 251

Principles for Organizing Serenity Groups or Celebrations 253

Group Journey Guides and Workbook.................................. 257

The Twelve Steps of Alcoholics Anonymous............................ 259

About the Author... 261

Recommended Reading 263

The Prayer Steps Power Pack 267

The Twelve Steps and Prayer

The Counselor, the Holy Spirit, whom the Father will send in my name, will teach you all things and will remind you of everything I have said to you. Peace I leave with you; my peace I give you. I do not give to you as the world gives. Do not let your hearts be troubled and do not be afraid.
—John 14:26-27

It is easy to let up on the spiritual program of action and rest on our laurels. We are headed for trouble if we do . . . What we really have is a daily reprieve contingent on the maintenance of our spiritual condition. Every day is a day when we must carry the vision of God's will into all of our activities.
—*Alcoholics Anonymous*, "The Big Book," page 85

God is with you and for you. After working through The Twelve Steps in A.A., Al-Anon, Serenity Groups, or some other recovery program, many of us came to realize that God went before us and with us every Step of the way. We now see that a loving, caring

God came and convinced us that we were powerless over many of the problems, people, situations, sicknesses, addictions, compulsions, dependencies, weaknesses, or sins that beset us. When we began to follow the God-given Program in The Twelve Steps, we met others who had found relief and recovery one Step at a time, one day at a time. By praying, trusting in God, and walking The Twelve Steps Journey, we found serenity. Continuing to pray The Serenity Prayer and living our lives on the spiritual foundation of The Twelve Steps brought us success in a "program of action."

Through the indwelling Holy Spirit, God is our ever-present Counselor. God wants to give us the Power we lack to change, working from the inside out. God wants to be the transforming Power for us and within us. When God's light broke through our darkness, we saw clearly that our lives had become unmanageable and out of control in areas that were leading us to destruction and destroying others and our relationships with them. Though we did not know it at the time, we actually craved an honest, loving, and open fellowship with God and others. Though we did not know of His continuing and loving presence, God was working in our lives as our Counselor and Guide to lead us to serenity and sobriety. He wanted to guide us in recovery and restore our cherished relationships.

Once convinced of our condition, we turned our lives over to God and received the peace and power of His presence within us. As we faced our character defects, our evil actions and destructive patterns of behavior, we confessed them (as painful as this was at the time). Through sincere confession, we found forgiveness. Once forgiven by our gracious God, we discovered that other human beings received the grace of God to forgive us too. With the forgiveness and support of God, we even learned how to forgive ourselves. What a joy when wholeness and health returned to us and to our relationships with God and others! We felt a peace beyond understanding as we kept our focus on God, Who helps us daily. In speaking to others, we have discovered that the best name for this lasting peace with God, others, and ourselves is Serenity. With God's help, we took a Twelve Steps Journey to serenity, joy, and lasting happiness.

God has graciously given us proven Steps to Serenity. By His grace, we can study daily and follow the necessary Steps to overcome our weaknesses, live victoriously, stay close to God, and achieve lasting joy. Time-tested Prayer Step Principles that will meet our every need can be key ingredients to recovery and serenity. Watch for the special Prayer Step Principles by various authors scattered throughout the book. God wants us to be in conscious contact with Him every day. He waits daily for us to spend time with Him—because He loves us and knows that prayer and daily communication with Him are our greatest needs each day. God wants us to invite Him into our lives so He can be our constant Comforter and Power. He wants to lead us daily in the paths of peace.

Prayer Steps to Serenity will help you work through The Twelve Steps and pray The Serenity Prayer more effectively no matter where you are in your recovery. Whether you are on your First Step or your Twelfth Step, or preparing to take your Fifth Step, your recovery will be more certain through the daily practice of the prayer principles in this book. If you find yourself only "two-stepping" (working only the First and Twelfth Steps), then *Prayer Steps to Serenity* will help you be honest with yourself, with God, with others, and help you work the total Twelve Steps Program.

Allow me to offer you a few suggestions to help you get the most from *Prayer Steps to Serenity*. (You may prefer to skip the rest of this chapter and go directly to the daily readings in this book. If so, please come back to this chapter before your second reading of *Prayer Steps to Serenity*.) You cannot completely understand and practice all that *Prayer Steps to Serenity* has to offer by reading through the book only once in a short period of time. Pray through the Prayer Steps. Let me repeat this with emphasis: *Pray through the Prayer Steps!* Pray after each day's reading. Complete the prayers in this book in your own words. Write your prayer requests in the space provided in this book.

Answer the questions in The Twelve Steps Journey Workbook for each of the 12 Steps as you read the book. Every time you pray through the book, you will climb higher and higher in your spiritual experience and understanding. As the illustrations in the book indicate, you will become like a growing, budding tree, coming to life after a cold winter to welcome the warmth of spring and summer. At harvest time, you will begin to bear much fruit and bless others with your life. God and others will rejoice in their relationship with you. You will look forward to your Twelfth Step work and be better prepared to do it. You will rejoice each day as you work the Twelfth Step, having completed successfully the first eleven Steps. Indeed, because God is with you and for you, *God will rejoice* in His relationship with you and you will bless God. You will rejoice everyday as you walk in the teachings of *Prayer Steps to Serenity: The Twelve Steps Journey*. By looking back from time to time as you step forward, you will learn to praise God for the progress you have made—one day at a time, one Step at a time. As you grow closer to God and grow in your understanding of God, write between the lines and in the generous margins of this book any new ideas or concepts that you discover from your study of each devotional reading. Share your new discoveries and ideas with those in your Fellowship or Serenity Group, with your family (if possible), with your friends, with others online, and with those who may be needing to work a Twelve Steps Program.

When you begin to pray through the early readings, you may not understand all the teachings in each day's devotional. However, if you will keep a daily or weekly record of your impressions, needs, and prayer requests as you walk in The Twelve Steps Journey, you will be able to look back and see the progress you have made through the Prayer Steps. Work through this book more than once. Create your own *Serenity Journal* by using a small notebook, by writing in each of The Twelve Steps Journey Workbook pages in this book, by downloading the Prayer Steps Journal pages online at PrayerSteps.org, by creating a Prayer Steps Blog to help others as well as yourself. Your record of recovery will give you an even greater assurance that God is walking with you as He does with so many who take the action this program prescribes. You will see how you have grown spiritually. You will have a written reminder of the key truths you have discovered on your journey, and you may be able to correct some of your initial impressions. As you continue walking in the Prayer Steps to Serenity, you will experience God revealing more truths for you to record in your personal *Serenity Journal* and for you to share with others at His prompting.

To deepen and improve your relationships with God and others, answer the questions in The Twelve Steps Journey Workbook as a weekly review and study of that week's Step and The Serenity Prayer. I added twelve new devotional readings to this *New Serenity Prayer Edition* of *Prayer Steps to Serenity: The Twelve Steps Journey*. Each of these readings relates one of The Twelve Steps to a small part of The Serenity Prayer. For example, "The First Step and The Serenity Prayer" reading will encourage you to contemplate how the First Step and the words "God, grant me" in The Serenity Prayer tie closely to one another. Meditating on the relationship between each Step and each part of The Serenity Prayer will help you in your daily praying through The Twelve Steps. If you will, right this moment, please pause in your reading and think about the difference between "God grant me" and "God, grant me" (notice the comma in the second option between God and grant). As you deepen your spiritual life, the difference will become more astounding. In *Prayer Steps to Serenity: The Twelve Steps Journey*, when I write The Serenity Prayer I will usually use the form "God, grant me" (with the comma between God and grant). After you read and pray through the devotional reading on The Serenity Prayer, you can begin The Twelve Steps Journey Workbook on that Step (or you may want to wait until later in the day to complete your workbook). Answer the questions in The Twelve Steps Journey Workbook. Reserve some extra Quiet Time that day, and work on completing that Step's Workbook questions some time during the day. Pour yourself a cup of coffee or tea, relax, and answer the questions for that Step in your Journey. During your Quiet Time, review your notes on the previous days, and think about what you need to practice in the week ahead—with God's help. Pray for God's guidance and power to help you in the coming days. Write your own devotional on the Step, and perhaps share it in your next Fellowship meeting, Serenity Groups meeting, with your friends, or online. You can walk the Prayer Steps to Serenity in twelve short weeks; however, practicing these Steps takes you on an exciting journey, a journey that brings rejoicing and serenity; a journey that lasts a lifetime—The Twelve Steps Journey.

Consider using *Prayer Steps to Serenity* as the basis for discussion and study in your support group or recovery meeting. All recovery group meetings should be strictly confidential among those attending. You will find additional support from sharing with others what you have learned from *Prayer Steps to Serenity*. Talk about your needs or the sources of your help. In your recovery or prayer support group, you might study each of The Twelve Steps during a twelve week or twelve month period. Use the Group Journey Guides in the back of *Prayer Steps to Serenity* as a basis for group sharing, support, and prayer. As ideas come to mind, write down additional questions or thoughts for discussion in your *Serenity Journal*. For more ideas on how to conduct a Recovery Journey or Serenity Group, see "Principles for Organizing Serenity Groups or Celebrations" on page 253, or go to PrayerSteps.org. Weekly meeting guides that you can print out and use as is, or edit in a word processor, are available at the official Serenity Groups web site at SerenityGroups.org and the Prayer Steps web site at PrayerSteps.org. If you would prefer to introduce others to the Prayer Steps to Serenity, but not use the official Twelve Steps (which might intimidate or offend some people), consider a study using *Prayer Steps to Serenity: Daily Quiet Time Edition* (the abridged edition of this book). Following that study, some might see their need to work through the official Twelve Steps in *Prayer Steps to Serenity: The Twelve Steps Journey*.

In your support or prayer group, some may not want to share all their answers in The Twelve Steps Journey Workbook or their writings in their *Serenity Journal*. Respect their need for privacy. If you use *Prayer Steps to Serenity* to begin a prayer group or support group in your church or home, before the meeting begins be certain to remind those attending of the important principle of confidentiality. We have found that inclusive Serenity Groups encourage people with one or more problems to feel comfortable learning how to apply and discuss The Twelve Steps Journey without feeling compelled to reveal the exact nature of their weaknesses or wrongs to the group. If you cannot find a support group near you, visit the Serenity Groups web site at SerenityGroups.org for help and information. Consider forming a *Prayer Steps Group* or *Serenity Group* in your church or community. Think about and pray for God's leading in your starting a *Prayer Steps Group* that could meet for coffee and fellowship immediately before or following your regular A.A., Al-Anon, NA, EA, CoDA, OA, Overcomers Outreach, church, or other recovery group meeting. *Prayer Steps to Serenity* was not written to replace your current recovery program. The principles taught in this book will give you greater power through prayer to work your program, succeed in your recovery, help others, find lasting joy, maintain your serenity, and work The Twelve Steps.

A few in your recovery group or family may express hostility toward you and your spiritual convictions if you express them openly too soon. You must make this a matter of prayer, and the principles in *Prayer Steps to Serenity: The Twelve Steps Journey* will help you deal wisely in love with these less understanding people and groups. God can break through to those who are hateful toward Him or angry with those He has touched spiritually and healed substantially. In dealing with some, you must make them the object of your First Step: "We admitted we were powerless over (name of person or group)—that our lives had become unmanageable (in relation to them)." You cannot change, control, or manage their lives. You must not let them influence you to become unmanageable in your attitudes or actions. Pray! God will give the victory! God achieves marvelous things and changes lives when believers pray. If some still refuse to invite God into their lives or follow His ways, then God will grant you the serenity to accept the things (or people) you cannot change and the wisdom to know the difference.

Please, do not think that you must complete each Step of The Twelve Steps during the week it takes to read the seven devotional readings and answer The Twelve Steps Journey Workbook questions. Working through the whole book once will give you an overview of what God *can* do through prayer and The Twelve Steps. Your first reading will encourage you to keep on working through The Twelve Steps and praying The Serenity Prayer wherever you are in your recovery. Some people with several years of recovery behind them—one day at a time—have needed many months to work on each Step before feeling ready for the next one—so don't get discouraged! As you cooperate with God by putting Prayer Steps principles into daily practice, you will achieve recovery more quickly and with greater permanence and stability than if you did not maintain a conscious relationship with God. You can experience joy and serenity each day of your life by practicing what you learn through this book.

To avoid or overcome those sometimes lengthy periods that some label "the dry drunk," "darkness of the soul," or "spiritual depression," go back and pray through *Prayer Steps to Serenity: The Twelve Steps Journey* again. Practice the principles you have been omitting in your relationship with God and others. Look for something new in the Prayer Steps that you missed or did not understand earlier. If you seek God's help daily, God will reveal new light to you regarding how to overcome your problems and weaknesses with His power. He will restore your happiness. Discuss your needs with your Serenity Group and learn how God and prayer have helped them. Share your needs in one of the discussion forums at PrayerSteps.org and ask others to pray for you.

After you have read each daily devotional, write your own meditations, prayers, and prayer requests. Make your prayer requests as specific as possible, so when God answers your prayers, He can also strengthen your faith and encourage you to develop daily your relationship with Him. Given enough time, you may discover why God has chosen *not* to grant you a specific prayer request. God will show you His love, wisdom, and concern by *not* giving you things or relationships that are not helpful or that you are not yet ready to receive. God invites us to come to Him day-by-day with our requests, and He wants to give us what we need day-by-day. From time to time, review your prayer requests and wherever you can add the date that God answered your prayer. Praise God for the answers you receive. If you ever feel discouraged, go back and praise God for these "dated" answers. God's faithfulness to you in answering your prayers will give you the encouragement you need.

Jesus taught us to pray, *"Give us this day our daily bread."* Every time God answers our prayers, His Spirit stirs our hearts to praise Him and love Him more. As you pray through The Twelve Steps, The Serenity Prayer, and *Prayer Steps to Serenity*, you will learn more about why God answers some of our prayers with a "Yes" and others with a "No" or "Not Yet." As we wait day-by-day for some answers from God, God will teach us patience and help us develop the other character traits that we need to overcome our weaknesses, rejoice always, and find serenity. In our *Serenity Journal*, we need to record the "No" answers as well as the "Yes" answers to our prayers, so we can learn to praise God for them both. As we grow in our understanding of God's wisdom, we will discover why the answer must sometimes be "No" and why "No" is sometimes best. Through daily experience with God in prayer, we will learn to trust Him even more when the answer is "No" or "Not Yet." We will not lose our serenity when God delays a "Yes" answer from our point of view. God is not like a mechanical gum ball machine or slot machine, "a one-armed bandit" that holds out the promise of a rare win after countless loses. God really cares for us. As God guides us to pray according to His will, He will give us only what is best for others and us. Learning this key lesson will go a long way toward helping us achieve and maintain serenity. As you learn more about why God answers some prayers and some people more than He appears to answer others, your prayers will change and you will discover God answering more of your prayers with a "Yes" than a "No." Eventually, you may come to understand God's will so perfectly that you will always pray according to His will at all times and always receive a "Yes" answer to your prayers. Watching God work in answer to your prayers and the prayers of others will inspire you to rejoice in God daily and give you sound reasons for the serenity you enjoy.

You may find it helpful to practice writing out your own prayers of praise or your own deepest desires, longings, confessions, weaknesses, or needs. You may want to use the brief prayers at the end of each daily devotional as a "starter" prayer for you. The "Prayer for Today" does not end with an "Amen." The "dots" are placed at the closing of the prayer to encourage you to keep on praying and complete your requests in your own words. Pray for the Holy Spirit to help you complete the prayer idea or sentence at the end of each "Prayer for Today." Perhaps your prayers will relate to that day's reading or to an answer to prayer that you have received. Encourage others by sharing your prayers in a group meeting or online forum. Keep a record of your prayers in your *Recovery Journal* or *Serenity Journal*. You can maintain your serenity in times of trouble by reviewing your written prayers and your record of God's work in your life.

Remember, write down and date your prayer requests at the end of each reading or study. After God answers a prayer, record the date and answer in your journal or in this book. Make time to review periodically your prayer requests. In times of deepest discouragement, when you are tempted to give up, God's answers to the prayers that you have recorded, or the prayers of a better time, will encourage you to keep on going *"from strength to strength"* (Psalm 84:7) throughout your Twelve Steps Journey. Review and review again. Ask yourself if God has already answered some of your prayer requests. Have you not realized that God has given you what is best under the circumstances? Are any of your requests now irrelevant because of the changes you have experienced in your own spiritual growth? We need to examine ourselves to see where God has made us stronger in certain areas, so we will know that we are overcoming our weaknesses with His strength and guidance. Think of various ways that you can help others; share with them your answers to prayer and what you have learned about prayer. Pray for them and add their prayer requests to your prayers when you can. Follow up with them, and add their answers to your Prayer Journal or write them in this book.

If you give this book to others who might enjoy learning the prayer principles found in *Prayer Steps to Serenity*, share with them how the book has helped you. If they do not need to be involved in a recovery program (or do not know they need to find a program suited to their problems), assure them of the book's value. You may feel that you should gently introduce them to the principles of *Prayer Steps to Serenity* by giving them the new abridged edition *Prayer Steps to Serenity: Daily Quiet Time Edition*. Tell them that you do not mean to imply "You really need this book!" After reading this book in its earlier edition, some found the courage to enter recovery programs and treatment centers. They found a measure of serenity, and they knew they needed to move forward in their recovery by seeking professional treatment or going to A.A. meetings. They knew that God would go with them. They felt comfort from knowing that the prayers of their family and friends would be with them. They gained the wisdom and the courage to take the risk of recovery. They stepped out in a journey of faith toward peace with God, others, and themselves that we call "The Twelve Steps Journey." *Prayer Steps to Serenity* can help others learn how to pray for you more specifically to overcome your weaknesses, and you can learn how to pray more effectively for others, even as you and those you love learn how to live more victoriously through prayer.

You may never know when you have met someone's personal needs by giving them one of the new editions of *Prayer Steps to Serenity*. Someday, they may thank you for leading them to work The Twelve Steps. If someone truly needs help, pray for the Holy Spirit to use this book to guide them to the help they need. Perhaps they have been praying for God's guidance and comfort, and will feel that receiving *Prayer Steps to Serenity* was an answer to their prayers. Those who read and share this book and its principles with others can make a difference in our world.

By reading *Prayer Steps to Serenity*, those who already love Bible Study and prayer will discover how the truths of the Scriptures can help people no matter how serious their problems or how complicated their needs. Believers can study this book to learn more about the power of prayer, the power of the Word of God, and the power of God's Spirit. Through diligent study, they can prepare themselves to share the Bible's teachings more effectively with everyone.

I hope you will study this book several times so you can recognize the progress you are making and give God all the love, praise, and glory for your recovery or for your improved ability to cope with those you cannot control. You will gain new insights and understanding each time you read and pray through *Prayer Steps to Serenity: The Twelve Steps Journey*. You will learn more about the God of the Bible and His Son, Jesus Christ, Who died to save you from your sins and weaknesses, Who will forgive you and cleanse you from your sins, and Who will open the way to eternal life for you. You will come to know personally the Holy Spirit, Who will become your daily Comforter, Counselor, Friend, Guide, and indwelling Power. Perhaps you have only heard these facts about God very vaguely or have even rejected them in the past. If so, read *Prayer Steps to Serenity* with an open mind and heart to discover what these truths about God can mean to you. You may discover the true God and come to know God personally for the first time in your life as you study this book and learn to pray more effectively.

If you personally do not need a recovery program, thinking through The Twelve Steps and practicing what you learn in *Prayer Steps to Serenity* will empower you to help others no matter what their need. In *Prayer Steps to Serenity: Daily Quiet Time Edition*, an abridged edition of this book, I have presented The Twelve Steps in a way that does not explicitly resemble a recovery program, and this may be the best way to introduce The Twelve Steps to some people. By taking the Prayer Steps in either edition, you will draw closer to God, better understand the Scriptures in a practical way, and be prepared to help others with a better knowledge of The Twelve Steps of recovery. If you are unfamiliar with The Twelve Steps, read "The Twelve Steps of Alcoholics Anonymous" in this book on page 259. If you only want a Quiet Time book that does not work through The Twelve Steps precisely, then you might enjoy *Prayer Steps to Serenity: Daily Quiet Time Edition* for those not interested in working a Twelve Steps Program, but who want to learn some of the Prayer Steps to Serenity in this book.

If you have enjoyed *Prayer Steps to Serenity*, and have found it helpful, you will also want to read *How to Pray in the Spirit* by John Bunyan and *Principles of Prayer* by Charles G. Finney (compiled and edited by L.G. Parkhurst, Jr.). If you have come to know God more deeply, or have received Jesus Christ as your Lord and Savior while reading this book, please let us know. If we may assist you in other ways, contact us through the Information Form on PrayerSteps.org or SerenityGroups.org or send me a personal e-mail to lgpjr@prayersteps.org.

Prayers in the Program

From the beginning of Alcoholics Anonymous and the various Twelve Steps Programs that began after A.A., prayer played an important role in recovery. The original version of The Serenity Prayer was written by Reinhold Neibuhr. His daughter, Elisabeth Sifton, wrote a delightful account of the original prayer in "The Serenity Prayer," *The Yale Review*, New Haven, January 1998, pages 16-65. Her father wrote the prayer and first read it publicly in the Heath Union Church (Congregational), Heath, Massachusetts, in the summer of 1943, at the height of World War II. Dean Robbins, who heard the prayer in that summer service, included it in the 1944 edition of *Book of Prayers and Services for the Armed Forces, Prepared by the Commission on Worship of the FCC and the Christian Commission for Camp and Defense Communities*. The FCC is the old Federal Council of Churches. Elisabeth Sifton said that her father was happy to have his prayers used in whatever context people wanted or needed them. She reproduced "The Original Serenity Prayer" on page 16 of her article in *The Yale Review*. See also her book, *The Serenity Prayer: Faith and Politics in Times of Peace and War* by Elisabeth Sifton, W. W. Norton & Company, October, 2003—ISBN: 0393057461 (hardback) and ISBN: 0393326624 (paperback).

The Original Serenity Prayer

God, give us grace to accept with serenity the things

that cannot be changed,

courage to change the things that should be changed,

and the wisdom to distinguish the one from the other.

By Reinhold Neibuhr

The "Complete" Serenity Prayer

From time to time, various versions of The Serenity Prayer claim to be the "Complete" version. These prayers are not by Reinhold Neibuhr, but a common example of one of them is reprinted below.

God, grant me the Serenity

To accept the things I cannot change

Courage to change the things I can

And the Wisdom to know the difference.

Living one day at a time;

Enjoying one moment at a time;

Accepting hardship as the pathway to peace.

Taking, as He did,

this sinful world as it is,

not as I would have it.

Trusting that He will make all things right,

if I surrender to His Will;

That I may be reasonably happy in this life,

and supremely happy with Him forever in the next. Amen.

The Third Step Prayer
Alcoholics Anonymous, "The Big Book," page 63.

GOD, I offer myself to Thee—

to build with me and to do with me as Thou wilt.

Relieve me of the bondage of self, that I may better do Thy will.

Take away my difficulties, that victory over them may bear

witness to those I would help of Thy Power, Thy Love, and

Thy Way of life.

May I do Thy will always!

The Seventh Step Prayer
Alcoholics Anonymous, "The Big Book," page 76.

My Creator, I am now willing that you should have all of me,

good and bad.

I pray that you now remove from me

every single defect of character which stands in the way

of my usefulness to you and my fellows.

Grant me strength, as I go out from here, to do your bidding.

Amen.

Day 1
The First Step to Serenity

We admitted we were powerless to overcome our weaknesses—that our lives had become unmanageable.
—The First Step

Yet the LORD longs to be gracious to you; he rises to show you compassion. For the LORD is a God of justice. Blessed are all who wait for him!
—Isaiah 30:18

To take the First Step, I need to humble myself. I need to admit that I am powerless over my weaknesses, perhaps a weakness toward alcohol or the alcoholic. Perhaps I am a slave to some other addiction or compulsion, or some sinful habit that I cannot seem to break. More than this, I need to recognize what my behavior indicates: I am not managing my life very well by myself. Perhaps others have been telling me this repeatedly, but I have refused to listen. Perhaps I have been too proud to admit they were right. Perhaps I have not wanted to admit to myself that I cannot control every area of my life. I do not want to face the fact that I do not have the will power to "Just Say No." In the First Step, I only need to admit these things to myself. When I take the First Step, I go a long way down the road to recovery. An old Greek proverb says, "Well begun is half done."

I may not be ready to accept these truths yet, but God is giving grace to me in my weaknesses. God will show me even more of His compassion when I begin to admit to myself my true condition. God loves to be strong where I am weak! Even though God is a God of justice, He is full of mercy and looks for ways to display His mercy. God loves me and seeks to lead me back to fully trusting in Him. Practicing the Prayer Steps to Serenity will help me depend on His guidance and power instead of my trying to run my life all by myself.

When I admit that I am not God, I open the door for God's help. I need to confess my self-centeredness and selfishness. I need to see that focusing primarily on myself has failed me. I need to face the fact that my life is out of control and uncontrollable in certain key areas. I may be able to function fine at work, but I need to face the fact that in many other areas I am hurting others and myself by my behavior. Others at work might think that there is nothing wrong with me, because I have learned how to cover things up and fool them. However, my family and closest friends might be suffering daily from my uncontrolled weaknesses and excesses. My hostility and anger (which may be more self-directed than toward those I am hurting) may be out of control around those I love. I need to humble myself. I need to admit *to myself* what those closest to me probably already know about my weaknesses and the nature of my wrongs.

I need to prayerfully step down the road of humility to find God and receive God's help. John Bunyan wrote:

> *He that is down, needs fear no fall;*
> *He that is low, no loss of pride.*
> *He that is humble ever shall*
> *Have God to be his Guide.*

Amazingly, when I humble myself before God, God will not push me further down. God exercises His justice with love, and God promises to lift up the humble and be gracious to them. Saint Augustine wrote about pride and humility: "Pride changed angels into devils; it is humility that makes us into angels." Someone once said of God, "His business is to lift up the humble and cast down the proud." I thank God for His tireless efforts to make and keep me humble! His love motivates His efforts to help me see myself as I truly am. I can begin admitting to Him and to myself my true situation and real needs in life.

As I work through the First Step with prayer, God will quickly lead me to a true estimate of myself—the real meaning of humility. God will speak to my heart and personally assure me of His guidance and power to help me (and others) change. Furthermore, His love will uphold me whenever I face things or people that will not change in this life. Thankfully, through faith in Jesus, I know that I will be made whole in the life to come. In eternity, He will heal all of my relationships with His infinite love. However, I must not wait until then to take action. Some things can change now, for God can give me substantial healing, strength, and joy in this life when I pray with trust in Him,

Prayer for Today

God, grant me the Serenity to accept the things I cannot change, the Courage to change the things I can, and the Wisdom to know the difference. Lord God, help me today to . . .

Prayer Step Principle

You will keep him in perfect peace, whose mind is stayed on you: because he trusts in you.

—Isaiah 26:3 in the *King James Version*

Day 2
The Source of All My Power

We admitted we were powerless to overcome our weaknesses—that our lives had become unmanageable.
—The First Step

I am the vine; you are the branches. If a man remains in me and I in him, he will bear much fruit; apart from me you can do nothing.
—John 15:5

Because of pride, we can proudly begin to think that we are making ourselves better and do not need anyone else. Yet, apart from God, we are powerless. Without God, we do not have the power to do anything good, either for others or ourselves. Without God, our weaknesses will always defeat us. In fact, apart from God, we only fight against God, others, and even ourselves. Without God's help, we are unwilling to make the necessary and needed changes in our lives.

Jesus truly offers to change our lives and bless us when He promises, "apart from me you can do nothing." We need to remember that apart from Jesus we cannot even pray or go to God for help. Apart from Jesus we are not able to discern God's purposes or receive the power to achieve God's will for our lives.

Today, I have many good reasons to give thanks. For one, Jesus promises that when I come to Him, for Him to direct my life, He will unite himself with me. He will dwell within me and never leave me. I need to admit that I cannot manage every area of my life perfectly. In some areas, I just feel powerless to do the right thing, even when I know the right thing to do. When I ask Jesus to give me power to change so I can bless others, He will. Through daily prayer, meditation on the Scriptures, and obedience, I can open my life to Him. Then, He will be able to live in me, to work in me, and to work through me each day—all day long. I may be powerless all by myself, but God's power will work in me and through me.

I have good reason for continuous joy and encouragement—the Lord Jesus can work in me! I need to remind myself daily that without God I am powerless. I need to depend on Him to care for me, and work through me all the day, one day at a time—sometimes moment-by-moment. Whenever I recall that Jesus promised, "apart from Me, you can do nothing," I need to remember Jesus' other promise, "The one who abides in Me bears much fruit." I want to start bearing much good fruit to bless the lives of others, especially those whose lives I have been hurting through my selfish or self-centered behavior. I will abide in Christ, and share His love with others. In Christ, I will bear much good fruit. I will believe His promises. Today, I will trust in Him as I pray and receive the love He has for me.

Prayer for Today

Dear God, help me to remember that without you my life is uncontrollable. When I try to do well, I too often fail. Do not let me forget that I am powerless to overcome many things, and that apart from you I can do no good thing. Take control of my life and help me to change. Grant me the serenity your presence brings. Give me power to overcome the weaknesses I feel today. Today, help me overcome . . .

Day 3
The Good Fight of Faith

We admitted we were powerless to overcome our weaknesses—that our lives had become unmanageable.

—The First Step

Fight the good fight of the faith. Take hold of the eternal life to which you were called when you made your good confession in the presence of many witnesses.

—1 Timothy 6:12

When I try to pray in my own strength, I am always disappointed and discouraged. However, I have found a struggle that leads to victory. The Bible speaks of it as "the good fight of faith." This fight springs from within me, and I can carry it on by faith. When I get the right understanding of faith, I can stand unmoved in faith. I can achieve the victory I seek over my addictions and compulsions.

Jesus is the Author and Finisher of my faith. The Bible gives me encouragement with these words: "Let us fix our eyes on Jesus, the Author and Finisher of our faith, who for the joy set before him endured the cross, scorning its shame, and sat down at the right hand of the throne of God" (Hebrews 12:2). When I enter into a right relationship with Jesus, He assures me of His help and power in prayer each moment of every day. The work that He has begun in me He will bring to completion for He is also the Author and Finisher of my faith in Him.

To receive God's help, I need to say in my heart, "I cannot strive in my own strength and succeed. In my own strength, I have failed again and again. I will cast myself before Jesus. I will wait on Him in the certain confidence that He will be with me and will work in me. I know that He can help me overcome all of my temptations and weaknesses with His power working in me." I need to commit myself to Him and resolve within myself to strive in prayer. I will work at prayer. Prayer will become the essential part of my "program of action" that lasting recovery requires. I will let faith fill my heart. Through faith, I will be strong in the Lord in the power of His might.

I always need to remind myself that I do not need to fight this fight alone. I have discovered what many have learned by experience: "I labor, struggling with all His energy, which so powerfully works in me" (Colossians 1:29). Jesus Christ will work in me when I trust in Him. I struggle to overcome my difficulties. I labor to bless others with my words and actions. Yet, it is the power of Jesus Christ in me that gives me the energy and power I need to overcome all of my obstacles and win the victory in Him. He will finish what He has begun. Today, I want Him to take over the management of my life and give me the power to achieve what I cannot achieve apart from Him. I will experience true joy as I pray and give more of my life over to His control.

Prayer for Today

This day, dear God, strengthen my faith in you and in your only begotten Son, Jesus. By your Holy Spirit, give me the assurance that you have adopted me into your family, and grant me serenity. As one of your dear children, reassure me when I doubt. Increase my faith in you. Be my strength and shield. Be with me always and be my guide. Take control over every area in my life that has become unmanageable. Today, please take control now over . . .

Day 4
The Right Attitude in Prayer

We admitted we were powerless to overcome our weaknesses—that our lives had become unmanageable.

—The First Step

I have fought the good fight, I have finished the race, I have kept the faith.

—2 Timothy 4:7

If my heart is cold and dark as I begin to pray, I cannot force myself into a right attitude. All I can do in these times is bow before God and honestly let Him see my real condition. I need to remind Him and myself that He is my only hope. With a childlike trust, I can trust Him to have mercy upon me. I have nothing—He has everything.

I have found that faith in the love of Jesus Christ is the only way I can get into fellowship with God in prayer. I remind myself of His love for me when I recite from memory: "For God so loved the world that he gave his one and only Son, that whoever believes in him shall not perish but have eternal life" (John 3:16). Reading the Bible will open the door for me to hear God's welcome invitation to come into His presence, pray, and have everlasting fellowship with Him. The Holy Spirit will fill me with the love of God when I seek fellowship with Jesus Christ through prayer and reading the Scriptures. The Holy Spirit will also give me the wisdom to understand the truth of God in the Bible and guide me in my daily decisions. The Holy Spirit will give me a right relationship with God through faith in Jesus Christ, a sense of well-being, peace, and joy.

I fight two spiritual battles. In the first battle, I must try to conquer my spirit of prayerlessness by ceasing to trust in my own strength. To win this fight, I need to give up my restless efforts and fall helpless at the feet of my loving Lord Jesus. He will speak the word, and my soul will live. He will speak the word to me through the Scriptures I read and those I remember by heart. He knows my needs and helps me.

Winning the second battle requires me to be deeply earnest. I need to exercise all the power God gives me to overcome my weaknesses. Through searching prayer, I watch over my heart. I pray for God to reveal to me the least moral or spiritual weaknesses in my life. I ask Him to help me overcome any proneness I have to disobey Him whenever I am tempted.

Above all, to have the right attitude in prayer, I need to surrender to God and live a life of personal self-sacrifice. Jesus sacrificed His life for me. I can do no less. If I seek to save my life, I will lose it, but if I lose my life for His sake, I will gain it. God really takes delight when He sees this attitude within me. If I surrender to Him, He will work out all things for my good. He will give me the victory over self and selfishness that separates me from Him and others. Today, in prayer, I will surrender myself to Him once again: something I have found I must do daily.

Prayer for Today

Dear Jesus, help me take all the time I need to wait on you in prayer. Fill my heart with your peace. I surrender all that I am, all that I have, and all that I hope to be to you. I do not have the power or the faith in myself to overcome my selfishness or my self-centered prayers and have serenity. I want to pray rightly, so cleanse me now and fill me with your Holy Spirit, who will pray rightly in me and for me. Today, cleanse me now from . . .

Day 5
God Meets Me in My Defects

We admitted we were powerless to overcome our weaknesses—that our lives had become unmanageable.

—The First Step

Now to him who is able to do immeasurably more than all we ask or imagine, according to his power that is at work within us, to him be glory in the church and in Christ Jesus throughout all generations, for ever and ever! Amen.

—Ephesians 3:20, 21

How prone I am to slide backward in my recovery and deliverance from my weaknesses and sins! I find it easy to give in to my addictions and compulsions. I limit God's power. I begin to think that God cannot do greater things. I have such limited concepts of God's promises, power, and personality! Too often, when I have failed, I have blamed God and others. When I have been powerless, I have thought God has been helpless. When my life has been out of control, I have accused God of incompetence. When considering my needs, I have sometimes denounced God for being a poor provider.

I need to ask God to make His real nature and character known to me. Each day, I need to admit that I am powerless to overcome my difficulties. To find real help, I need God as God really is. The god of my imagination is not present to help me. God gave us His name and revealed himself to us as: "I Am, Who I Am" or "I Am, Who I Will Be" (Exodus 3:14). The true God is the God we need. As I read the Scriptures, and as I share fellowship with God and other believers, I will learn more about God. The true God loves me, comes to me, saves me, and gives me good success.

I need to know by experience that God is all-powerful. In daily prayer and study of the Bible, I can learn the glorious truth that God is the All-Sufficient One. If I wait on His Spirit, God will open my heart to understand His promises and my real needs. The Comforter will help me see what great things God will give me in answer to prayer.

God really longs to bestow new and better things on those who pray to Him. Can I believe this today? Can I face the truth about myself? Can I face the real nature and character of God, a holy and loving God? Can I admit that I have character defects, but God has none? Can I admit that I am weak, but God is strong?

I need a deep and soul-searching humility in my prayer life. As my self-confidence decreases, my God-confidence must increase, or I will become more hopeless, weak, and defeated. God wants me to trust in His loving omnipotence. He wants me to pray with an increasing and believing boldness that comes from trust in Him and His promises. He wants me to express my great need for deliverance in the faith that He will graciously save me from destruction and help me overcome all my weaknesses. Because God loves me, I will pray boldly today, not with self-confidence, but with God-confidence.

Prayer for Today

Dear Jesus, in my strength I did not know you, but in my defects I have met you at the point of my greatest need. Today, give me your powerful presence so I can rest in your loving arms. Today, please help me to . . .

The First Step to
Serenity

Day 6
God's Power Can Fill My Emptiness

We admitted we were powerless to overcome our weaknesses—that our lives had become unmanageable.

—The First Step

I pray also that the eyes of your heart may be enlightened in order that you may know the hope to which he has called you, the riches of his glorious inheritance in the saints, and his incomparably great power for us who believe. That power is like the working of his mighty strength.

—Ephesians 1:18, 19

No matter how weak and powerless I feel, I need to remember that the almighty power of God will work within me and never fail me. I need to remind myself that God is almighty over all, and there is no power greater than God. With God's help I can overcome the power of any addiction, compulsion, or dependency.

While maintaining my trust in God's almighty power, God helps me accept the fact that I am powerless to overcome my addictions, dependencies, misbehaviors, temptations, weaknesses, and sins all by myself. He helps me accept the fact that by His power I can change and become the person God wants me to become and the person I truly want to become. God expects me to admit that I do not totally control my own destiny. I need to realize that the Holy and Loving God of the Scriptures is the only Person I can trust to rule my life effectively. As I trust in His love and generosity, God wants me to experience the joy and serenity that comes from His presence as He takes control of my life.

If I will only believe in God's willingness to work in me, He will give me a daily share in the resurrection power of His Son. Our Heavenly Father connected the resurrection of Jesus with the wonder-working power of God, by which He raised Jesus Christ from the dead. Such power God seeks to bestow upon me daily, if I will only admit my need of Him in prayer. Such power will sustain me in living for God—one day at a time.

With the beginning of each new day, I need to prayerfully and humbly confess my weakness and God's strength. Through this confession, I can have the confidence I need in the power of Jesus Christ to redeem me and restore my joy and serenity. If I trust God in prayer, God will fill me with His peace. God will give me confidence that His power in Jesus will give me the victory when I am tempted. He will give me peace beyond all expectation or understanding.

In my prayer fellowship with God, the Holy Spirit can fill me with the joy and victory that God won in the resurrection of Jesus Christ. In the midst of my temptations and trials, when I pray, Jesus will give me the power to overcome and succeed in life. May my meditations on the cross of Jesus Christ help me turn from sin and selfishness, so God can work in me by His mighty Spirit and bring life to me, even everlasting life.

Prayer for Today

Dear Heavenly Father, I may be so early into my recovery that I do not understand all you are trying to tell me about your power to overcome my weaknesses. I only see my failures. Even though I lack understanding, by your mighty Spirit work powerfully within me and set me free from every addiction or compulsion that I might grow in grace and comprehension for Jesus' sake. Today, increase my understanding of . . .

Day 7
The First Step and the Serenity Prayer

We admitted we were powerless to overcome our weaknesses—that our lives had become unmanageable.
—The First Step

God, grant me *the serenity to accept the things I cannot change, the courage to change the things I can, and the wisdom to know the difference.*
—The Serenity Prayer

Those who oppose him he must gently instruct, in the hope that God will grant them repentance leading them to a knowledge of the truth, and that they will come to their senses and escape from the trap of the devil.
—2 Timothy 2:25, 26

When we took the First Step we acknowledged that we were trapped in our addictive or compulsive behavior. After repeated efforts in our own strength to overcome our weaknesses, we recognized that we were powerless to achieve our goals. The Bible teaches that we can be trapped by the devil to do his will. In a similar way, we can be trapped by an addiction to alcohol, our drugs of choice, food, gambling, sex, other people or other behaviors; such as, lying, cheating, gossiping, not forgiving, hardness of heart, stealing, or slandering others. The devil can also work to keep us enslaved to harmful choices. God wants to free us from our sins, while the devil wants to keep us in bondage to him and lead us to destruction.

Thankfully, neither the devil nor our weaknesses need keep us in bondage. When the Bible says that gentle instruction and prayer to God can help us repent or turn around, we are encouraged to follow the Bible's teachings, to take the First Step, and to pray The Serenity Prayer. By praying The Serenity Prayer, we can enjoy personally and individually a conversation between "God" and "me." "God, grant me." When I pray The Serenity Prayer, I trust that God will grant me the freedom I seek and the serenity that will help me stay free from the traps that I have fallen into in the past.

When I completed the First Step and began praying The Serenity Prayer daily, I started a new life of striving for pure humility. I opened my eyes and ears to look and listen for what God wanted me to do. As I prayed and surrendered all that I knew about myself to God, He did His part and released me from the trap that was too strong for me to escape by myself. As God did His part, I responded by doing my part in following Him and The Twelve Steps Journey. Daily, I am admitting the fact that I cannot, but God can, so I am asking him to help me overcome my weaknesses.

When I pray, "God, grant me," I am admitting that I do not deserve His help. Precisely because I am powerless and my life has become unmanageable, precisely because I am unworthy to ask Him, God has promised me His love, grace, and mercy when I repent and turn to Him. In the First Step, I am completely giving up and not just asking God to fix a thing or two. In The Serenity Prayer, I am trusting in God to grant me a total life change as I trust in Him for deliverance. When I took the First Step, I admitted that when I tried to manage my life without relying on God that my life became unmanageable. When I pray The Serenity Prayer, I ask God to manage my life and give me the fruits of His labors and His Spirit, which are the Serenity, Courage, Change, and Wisdom I need each day.

Prayer for Today

Dear God, I am truly powerless to overcome my weaknesses. I have proven my powerlessness to myself by trying over and over again to help myself. Everything I have tried apart from you has failed. Therefore, I am admitting my weaknesses and powerlessness today, and I pray once again, "God, grant me the serenity to accept the things I cannot change, the courage to change the things I can, and the wisdom to know the difference." Help me now as I continue to pray and bring before you this day my greatest concern and fear . . .

Prayer Step Principle

The Holy Spirit prays for us by inspiring our minds. Not that He immediately suggests to us words, or guides our language, but He enlightens our minds and makes the truth take hold of our souls. He leads us to a deep consideration of the state of things, and the result of this is deep inspiration and yearning.

Charles G. Finney in *Principles of Prayer*

The Twelve Steps Journey
Step 1 Workbook

We admitted we were powerless to overcome our weaknesses—that our lives had become unmanageable.

—The First Step

For the foolishness of God is wiser than man's wisdom, and the weakness of God is stronger than man's strength.

—1 Corinthians 1:25

Things I have learned about God and prayer:

Things I have learned about myself:

What I have learned about my weaknesses:

What I have learned about others and my relationship with them:

My prayer requests and answers to prayer:

Prayer for Today

God, grant me the Serenity to accept the things I cannot change, the Courage to change the things I can, and the Wisdom to know the difference. Lord God, help me today to . . .

Day 8
The Second Step to Serenity

Came to believe that a Power greater than ourselves could restore us to sanity.

—The Second Step

Because Jesus himself suffered when he was tempted, he is able to help those who are being tempted.

—Hebrews 2:18

What strong, encouraging words I find in the Second Step: believe, power, and restore. Until I first believe, I will do nothing. When I come to believe, I open the door of my mind to receive the power I need to change and I begin to take action.

In the First Step, I discovered that believing could be painful. I painfully came to believe the truth about myself. How I hated to look myself in the mirror! In the Second Step, I joyfully believed and affirmed that a Power greater than myself could substantially heal my body, mind and spirit. Because God has restored so many in my Fellowship when they sought His guidance, I have good reasons to expect success when I take this next Step prayerfully as well.

The Bible gives many examples of what God can accomplish in the lives of people who believe and follow Him. Those I meet in my Fellowship also tell many stories about how a Power greater than themselves saved them from insanity or certain death. As I believe and trust more in God, I will find greater power in prayer, an almost miraculous, life-transforming power. Without faith, I can do nothing. From the Bible and the testimonies of people I meet, I can believe that God will do seemingly impossible things in my life.

Until I move beyond debating about God, I will not find sanity and serenity. I need to accept God as God has revealed himself. Debating is too close to justifying and rationalizing. I will not find healing until I put down my weapons, irrational objections, and believe. I need to encourage myself with the words of Jesus when He spoke to the parents of the twelve-year-old girl who had died before He reached her bedside and said: "Do not fear. Only believe, and she will be saved" (Luke 8:50). They believed. Jesus spoke the words, "Child, get up!" and she got up at once from her deathbed. Just as Jesus raised this girl from the dead when her spirit returned, I know that He can give me the power to overcome all of my unhealthy dependencies and the spiritual death I sometimes feel. I will trust in Him today. Through faith in Jesus, I will make more progress in The Twelve Steps Journey. My life will no longer contradict what I am coming to believe, and I will experience the restoration of my sanity. Today, I will pray that the Power greater than myself will restore my mind and spirit, and fill me with love and joy through believing.

Prayer for Today

God, grant me the Serenity to accept the things I cannot change, the Courage to change the things I can, and the Wisdom to know the difference. Lord God, help me today to . . .

The Second Step to
Serenity

Day 9
A Cure for My Anxiety

Came to believe that a Power greater than ourselves could restore us to sanity.

—The Second Step

Do not be anxious about anything, but in everything, by prayer and petition, with thanksgiving, present your requests to God.

—Philippians 4:6

Without God, I am lost. I cannot concentrate on my real needs or overcome my problems. I cannot even pray. I try one thing and then another, but either I fail or they fail me. I used to keep picking myself up, but now I am sick and tired of falling again and again. I need a Power greater than myself to give me healing, strength, and stability. I need the God-given joy and serenity that only God can give me in the midst of overwhelming troubles and worries.

God, help me to believe that only a real, continuous companionship with you will help me. Show me how prayer can become a daily life activity—moment by moment. I want my dependence on my Higher Power to be just as natural as breathing or sleeping, not something I use just once or more a day, like some drug or an instant fix.

Even though I do not see God face-to-face, I will follow the principle of completely depending on God for everything. I will develop the habit of remembering that He is present with me each moment of the day. Since God is always near, I can call upon Him at all times. Eventually, my experiences with God will give me many good reasons to keep on believing what the Bible teaches about not being anxious about anything.

I need to remember two things: God is always near me, with His infinite and abundant grace ready to overcome my problems. In addition, I am utterly frail, and I must call upon Him to give me the power I need. I want to give the holy, gracious God all the time I can, so His light, life and love will fill my whole life. If I give Him time, through His Word and prayer, His love and peace will abide in me every day. Today, I want to give God time, the time of life that He has given me, as I pray and develop a meaningful and everlasting relationship with Him.

Prayer for Today

Dear God, sometimes I find it difficult to believe that you will help me, or that I can ever find lasting serenity and peace. I have spurned your gracious offer of help for so long that I am not sure you will hear me now when I call. Yet, I have the testimony of others in my Fellowship, along with your Word, that you will help me. So, Lord, I am coming home. Today, help me leave behind . . .

Day 10
Overcoming My Greatest Stumbling Block

Came to believe that a Power greater than ourselves could restore us to sanity.

—The Second Step

Come to me, all you who are weary and burdened, and I will give you rest.

—Matthew 11:28

My greatest stumbling block was the feeling I could never change. Old habits, emotional attachments, and the attractions of my surroundings had a strong pull upon me. Whenever I thought victory was out of reach, I also thought, "Why try?" Now I recognize that the change I needed was too difficult for me to make alone, but I can make the change and God will help me make it.

Each day I need to ask God for the courage to believe that change and deliverance are possible for me. I need to ask Jesus for the courage to trust in Him. I need to tell Him that I am ready for Him to change me in any way He sees best. I must learn what total surrender means with respect to my relationship with God.

A defective spiritual life will lead to a defective prayer life. Lord Jesus, free me from the power of sin, and give me a life of true faith and prayer! Give me victory over my unbelief, and then give me the courage and power to change. Rather than follow the spirit of discouragement, I will place my faith in Jesus and choose to follow the spirit of gladness and hope.

God says to everyone in my Fellowship and to me: "Give yourself to me. Believe that I will help you pray. Believe that I will give you transforming power. I strongly seek to pour my love into your heart! Be conscious of your lack of power, and then rely upon me to give you grace and the power of prayer. I will cleanse you from all sin. I will deliver you from the sin of prayerlessness—only do not seek the victory in your own strength. Bow before me as one who expects everything from his Savior. However sad or discouraged you may be, be assured of this—I will be gracious and give you a trusting heart—I will teach you how to believe, pray, and change. I will give you serenity while the change you need takes effect in your life. I will walk with you each day as you walk The Twelve Steps Journey." Today, as I pray, I will expect more from God, as much as He wants me to expect as my faith grows in Him.

Prayer for Today

Dear Jesus, after trying so many ways to change and after saying so many prayers, I almost lost all hope. Once again, I need to let go—O God, change me. Give me all the power I need to recover from my troubles. Begin the healing I need today. As I wait on you, give me your peace and assurance. Today, give me the assurance that you will help me ...

The Second Step to
Serenity

Day 11
Jesus Makes Me New

Came to believe that a Power greater than ourselves could restore us to sanity.

—The Second Step

Therefore, if anyone is in Christ, he is a new creation; the old has gone, the new has come!

—2 Corinthians 5:17

For a long time I felt I had given God and Jesus a chance, but they had failed me. I was too impatient or too demanding, or I expected too much too quickly. I found that my whole approach to and relationship with Jesus, as my Lord and Savior, had to be entirely new. Where I had sat back passively waiting, I learned that I needed to take action.

First, I came to understand that because of His infinite love, Jesus really does seek to have communion with me every moment of the day. With all His heart, Jesus longs for me to enjoy His companionship. How amazing that He also wants to be my daily companion as my Friend and Brother.

Second, I came to believe in His divine power to conquer sin and keep me from falling. When I am tempted, if I look, I can find Him providing ways of escape for me and giving me the power I lack to follow Him out of trouble. With greater frequency, I now look to Jesus in prayer when I feel overpowering compulsions and temptations.

Third, since Jesus is the Great Intercessor, I now know that He will fill me with joy, and through the Holy Spirit He will give me the power to have daily communion with God in prayer. When I am in trouble, Jesus is praying in my behalf and His power will meet my needs and overcome my weaknesses. As my Divine Intercessor, He has foreseen my problems and prayed for me even before they started.

Fourth, I have discovered that when I awake each morning I need to come to Jesus and give my life and my day to Him once again. He will make me new each day. Therefore, at the dawning of every new day, I will ask Him to control completely my prayer life throughout the day.

My prayers are now becoming what God means them to be. Through the Spirit, my prayers are becoming the natural and joyful breathing of my spiritual life. In my communion and fellowship with Jesus, I now inhale the heavenly atmosphere and exhale my prayers to God. Prayer and obedience have become as natural to me as failing in my weaknesses used to be. Taking The Twelve Steps Journey has become a great joy and path of serenity for me! Today, I will rejoice as I pray and continue to grow in my relationship with God and receive His provisions for my problems.

Prayer for Today

Dear Jesus, take charge over me. Since you died for me, I can trust you and your love to guide me safely through life. Since God raised you from the dead for me, I know your power in me will be adequate for any situation. Teach me how to pray and remain in constant communion with you. Today, I pray that you will send your powerful presence when I . . .

The Second Step to
Serenity

Day 12
My Power from on High

Came to believe that a Power greater than ourselves could restore us to sanity.

—The Second Step

I am going to send you what my Father has promised; but stay in the city until you have been clothed with power from on high.

—Luke 24:49

Why does Jesus pay attention to weak, powerless, helpless people like me? Because He loves me and knows that when I yield to Him and give Him the opportunity to rule as Lord in my heart, He can show me His power to overcome in all things.

In the lives of His disciples, Jesus proved that His Father gave all power in heaven and on earth to Him. When Jesus sends the Holy Spirit to me as a powerful, personal presence within me, I cannot possess and use Him as I see fit or keep Him under my control. Just as Jesus lived and prayed on earth, so I need to pray, believe, and yield myself to the Father God so the mighty power of God will work in me too. Jesus found victory over temptation in this world through the power of the indwelling Holy Spirit, poured out upon Him by His Father, and so can I.

I want Jesus to make my whole attitude each day more prayerful, so His Spirit will influence me to lean with unceasing dependence upon Him. I need to pray daily with the confident expectation of receiving God's guidance and power in my life.

Jesus' first disciples saw Him love and heal the sick, cast out demons and raise the dead. They saw His power over everything. They saw Him still the raging storm and give them peace. They received His teaching and saw His sufferings. They saw Him in His power and in His seeming weakness. However, in His weakness, they saw the power of God in His life. They saw Him raised from the dead, and they experienced His resurrection power in their hearts. In His presence, their sorrows turned to joy.

They also learned that without His living presence and power in their hearts each day, they were not able to make the truth about Him known to others in the right way. From His throne in heaven, Jesus had to take possession of them by His Spirit and dwell within them through His Word. Jesus longs to do the same in my life, and all I need to do is maintain my daily, prayerful, obedient contact with Him. Today, I pray that as He fills me with His presence He will force out all selfishness still within me, so there will be nothing in my life that is withheld from Him and His influence.

Prayer for Today

Dear Jesus, overcome my unbelief and skepticism. You are the Creator and Sustainer of all that is. Help me rely on you as everything to me. Help me to yield myself totally to you, so I can know you personally as my Redeemer and Friend. Help me to be a true friend to you and others as you direct my steps. Today, I need your loving friendship more than I need . . .

Day 13
The Secret of My Power in Prayer

Came to believe that a Power greater than ourselves could restore us to sanity.

—The Second Step

If you love me, you will obey what I command. And I will ask the Father, and he will give you another Counselor to be with you forever—the Spirit of truth.

—John 14:15-17a

I will not be content with anything less than the indwelling life and power of the Holy Spirit in my heart. I cannot live reasonably and have the power to overcome my trials, troubles and temptations without Jesus working in me each day. Through daily prayer, I can know that He is with me and at work in my life.

If I want God to restore me to substantial wholeness, I need the same devotion to Jesus that I see in His first disciples. The Lord Jesus asks for this devotion from all those who desire that He fill them with the power of His Spirit. God desires to fill me and increase my capacity to receive His presence more fully each day. Moreover, He wants me to receive His Spirit and power so I can pray and intercede for others more effectively, to link my needs and the needs of others to the heart of God.

To some, Jesus is something or nothing. To me, Jesus is more than something. Jesus is everything to me! For those who do not know Him, Jesus is nothing. For the average believer, Jesus is something. For me, Jesus is everything. I will remind myself daily that Jesus is everything to me. To receive the power of the Holy Spirit, I need to pray each day: "Lord Jesus, I yield myself with my whole heart this day to the leading of the Holy Spirit." A full surrender, a total letting go and letting God, is a matter of life or death, sanity or insanity, joy or sorrow, an absolute necessity.

I have discovered that the mark of a true disciple is surrendering to God's love every day, all the day long. True discipleship involves abiding in the Lord Jesus Christ and keeping His commandments with a total reliance on His power and strength to help me love, trust and obey.

When I long to do God's will in everything, His love and Spirit rest upon me and give me joy and serenity. In this spirit and in His Holy Spirit, I always find my secret power in prayer. Today, as I think about my true needs and problems, I pray that God will help me trust more in Him and in His loving, all-sufficient power and presence in my life.

Prayer for Today

Dear God, I desperately need your power, and I need you: not just now in this time of need, but I need you every moment of the day. Teach me to pray and rely on your powerful presence in my life through Jesus' indwelling Spirit. Help me to face every challenge and trial with the serenity that overcomes stress. Today, since you are present in me and with me throughout each day, help me to win the victory when I am tempted to . . .

Day 14
The Second Step and the Serenity Prayer

Came to believe that a Power greater than ourselves could restore us to sanity.
—The Second Step

*God, grant me **the serenity** to accept the things I cannot change, the courage to change the things I can, and the wisdom to know the difference.*
—The Serenity Prayer

Teach me knowledge and good judgment, for I believe in your commands. Before I was afflicted I went astray, but now I obey your word.
—Psalm 119:66, 67

The dis-ease that many of us sometimes suffer can come from our inability or unwillingness to remain focused on God, our Higher Power, as the source of our serenity, our peace of mind. We need to keep reminding ourselves: "Trust God! Trust God! Trust God!" As we trust in God, our dis-ease gradually gives way to the calming presence of His Spirit within us.

We seek deliverance from the sometimes-insane situations we must cope with each day. We seek relief from the feelings of temporary insanity that make us feel a tempest is brewing in the calm spirit we want to maintain. Our turning to any unhealthy person, substance, or behavior that has promised temporary relief from our emotional pain has only made matters worse in the long term. We have finally discovered that the lasting sanity and serenity we need only comes from trusting in God and the good judgment He gives as we believe in His commands and obey His Word. God has been waiting for us to come to the end of "doing it ourselves." God invites us to turn to Him just as we are. God sincerely wants to help us, and He has offered tried and true guidance in the Bible. When we begin to obey His commands and trust in His Word, He begins to give us the sanity and serenity we have been seeking.

I can have peace, or a measure of peace, when I trust that God can do what I cannot do. The lesser powers that I have sometimes tried to use have truly hurt me. As I trusted in them, they abused me. I need to believe that peace from God, the Highest Power, is really possible for me. Just knowing that I can trust in God gives me peace. Truly trusting in God can help me find the peace I seek in every situation.

When I feel anxiety and I need my peace restored, I can pray The Serenity Prayer and trust in God as I pray. When I truly "pray" The Serenity Prayer (and not just repeat it from an unthinking memory), God gives me the peace that has eluded me. God grants me His answers to The Serenity Prayer in ways that seem absolutely astounding. I know He has the power to turn insanity to sanity, and give me a serenity that rests on sanity instead of destructive actions. Moving more and more toward sanity will give me a firmer and firmer grip on serenity and reality

We have discovered that sanity means wholeness. God *can* make me whole, but more importantly to me, God *wants* to make me whole and seeks to do so through the Holy Spirit that will indwell me when I invite Him into my life. If I have no recollection of sanity, of what it means to be sane, of a sanity to be restored to; then surely, God's blessings upon me will be new every morning and throughout the day. If I sincerely want to know what it looks like to live a sane life, I only need to read the gospels and learn how Jesus lived and treated others. I know I cannot become like

Jesus in my own strength, but He will give me the power I need to live like Him daily. He will tell me what to do and what to say through His Spirit in me. Today, I pray that I will feel His leading in my heart and hear His gentle voice giving me the guidance I need.

Prayer for Today

Dear God, through painful recollection, I know how powerless I am over my weaknesses, but I believe that you can help me—for you are all powerful and you are greater than I am. While I am weak, you are strong. O God, please bestow your peace upon me when I trust in you, your power, and your love to do for me what I cannot do; especially as I pray, "God, grant me the serenity to accept the things I cannot change, the courage to change the things I can, and the wisdom to know the difference." Help me now as I continue to pray and bring before you this day my greatest problems; for I know that you will give me the grace and power to overcome ...

Prayer Step Principle

True prayer is a sincere, sensible, affectionate pouring out of the heart or soul to God, through Christ, in the strength and assistance of the Holy Spirit, for such things as God has promised, or according to the Word of God, for the good of the Church, with submission in faith to the will of God.

John Bunyan in *How to Pray in the Spirit*

The Twelve Steps Journey
Step 2 Workbook

Came to believe that a Power greater than ourselves could restore us to sanity.

—The Second Step

I am not ashamed of the gospel, because it is the power of God for the salvation of everyone who believes.

—Romans 1:16a

Things I have learned about God and prayer:

Things I have learned about myself:

What I have learned about the way of believing:

What I have learned about others and my relationship with them:

My prayer requests and answers to prayer:

Prayer for Today

God, grant me the Serenity to accept the things I cannot change, the Courage to change the things I can, and the Wisdom to know the difference. Lord God, help me today to . . .

Day 15
The Third Step to Serenity

Made a decision to turn our will and our lives over to the care of God.
—The Third Step

But Christ said to me, "My grace is sufficient for you, for my power is made perfect in weakness." Therefore I will boast all the more gladly about my weaknesses, so that Christ's power may rest on me.
—2 Corinthians 12:9

The key words of action in the Third Step are decision, turn, and care. Through the success stories of others in my Fellowship and the examples in the Bible and other books, I see what great and wonderful things God can accomplish in those who have yielded their lives to His care. Eventually, I also need to decide to let go of myself and let God take control. After all, who better understands my needs than the One who created me with many good purposes in view for my life? No one can help me any better than the One who loves to indwell me.

God created me with the ability to choose, to originate my own choices. God has given me the ability to embrace or reject Him when He reaches out to me with His tender mercies. Left alone or in rebellion against authority, I will make decisions that will destroy my life and hurt others. However, God has the character, competence, and power to take control of my life in all matters. Therefore, to keep growing in His grace, I need to turn my freedom to choose over to Him. I do this in prayer. From my heart, I say to God, "I give up, you take over. Speak to me in the Bible, and I will listen. Show me what to choose, and I will choose it. Show me what to do and I will do it. Tell me how to act and I will act in your way."

Jesus taught that God cares for the birds of the air and the flowers in the fields and that He cares much more for people. After all, He created people in His own image. He cares for me now as I take these Prayer Steps, but I limit Him greatly if I continue to make choices contrary to His will and my best interests. Only God knows what is best for me, and He cares for me by showing me what is best in a variety of ways and through my Fellowship.

If I limit my understanding of God to my own imagination or to the ideas I have heard others share, I may not trust in the God who is there and who really wants to care for everyone, including me. Throughout my life, things have happened that have tended to warp my ideas about God. Therefore, as I prayerfully read the Bible and think about the ideas in the books I read and the opinions I hear, I need to pray and ask God to show me who He really is and what is true about Him. As I learn more about God, I can go joyfully to God each day in prayer, grateful that He will care for me as I turn that day over to His tender mercies and receive the peace and happiness God wants me to enjoy.

Prayer for Today

God, grant me the Serenity to accept the things I cannot change, the Courage to change the things I can, and the Wisdom to know the difference. Lord God, help me today to . . .

Day 16
Taking Time with God

Made a decision to turn our will and our lives over to the care of God.
—The Third Step

There is a time for everything, and a season for every activity under heaven.
—Ecclesiastes 3:1

God has given a time for everything—so why don't I spend more time in the presence of my Creator? Why don't I take the time to contemplate His will and purposes for me? Why not take time to measure my attitude and actions according to His revealed will in my reason, conscience, and the Scriptures?

My holy, loving God deserves the best of my time—of all my time. He merits the best in my life. I need to live in constant fellowship with God each day. To keep growing in faith, I must set aside a special Quiet Time to be alone with God, to ask Him to examine and improve my life.

I need a daily period for secret fellowship with God. I need a time for Him to shine the searchlight of His love into my heart, to reveal my hidden faults and intentions, the things I have done and left undone. I need time to turn daily from my occupations and search my heart in His presence. I need time to study His Word with reverence and godly fear. I need time to seek His face and ask Him to make himself known to me. I need time to wait until I know that He sees and hears me, so I can make my needs known to Him from the depth of my heart.

If I let God be God, and remember that I am only a creature, He will take the time to deal with my special needs. He will assure me of His forgiveness, cleanse me, and fill me with His mighty Spirit. If I let God take over the direction of my life, then God will show me what needs to be done and when to do it. If I let God take control of my daily decisions, then He will show me how to live and give me the power to have the victory I seek when my weaknesses would otherwise pull me away into destructive attitudes and behaviors.

Prayer for Today

Dear Father, I am so inclined to put everyone and everything else before you. Almost habitually I give you the time that I have left over, instead of putting you first and giving you my best time. Too often I give you my time at the close of a hectic day, when my mind is too exhausted to talk long with you. Until I put you first, I will never have serenity. Help me to overcome these faults by showing me the benefits of time spent with you for Jesus' sake. Today, as I spend time with you, I pray that you will take control over...

Day 17
Willing God's Will

Made a decision to turn our will and our lives over to the care of God.
—The Third Step

Going a little farther, Jesus fell with his face to the ground and prayed, "My Father, if it is possible, may this cup be taken from me. Yet not as I will, but as you will."
—Matthew 26:39

To abide in unbroken fellowship with Christ and maintain ceaseless prayer to God, I need to surrender my life to Him every day. I need to give myself over to His care and ask Him to help me die to sin, selfishness, and the unhealthy things of this world.

Only Jesus can teach me what it means to turn my life over to His care and have fellowship with His sufferings. When He agonized in prayer on Gethsemane, He looked forward to His death on the cross. He got such a vision of what it meant to die an accursed death under the power of sin that He prayed the cup might pass from Him. But when He heard again His Father's will, He yielded up His whole will and life to God in the words: "Thy will be done."

With these same words, "Thy will be done," I can enter into fellowship with God. With these words, Christ makes my heart strong and gives me confidence to believe that God will enable me, with Christ, to yield up everything to Him. I seek to be "crucified with Christ," to overcome my problems and inherit eternal life.

"Let God's will be done." May this bold declaration be the deepest and the highest thought in my life. In the love of Christ and in the power of His Spirit, may this definite daily surrender to the will of God become the joy and strength of my prayerful obedience. May I experience the serenity and true happiness that comes from a total submission to the will of God, a submission that resolves and repeats when tempted to do otherwise, "Let God's will be done." Today, in every prayer for help that I make, I will bow my heart before God and pray, "Not mine, but Thy will be done."

Prayer for Today

Dear Jesus, help me see that I need more than just a little course correction of my life. Today, I give my life completely over to you for your guidance and protection. Daily, help me to stop living only for myself. Turn me away from the self-centeredness that is destroying my life and serenity. Turn me to you so completely that I will be crucified with Christ each day and live in your power, wanting only your will for my life and the power to do it. Today, I pray for you to reveal your purposes for me so I can . . .

Day 18
From My Strength to God's

Made a decision to turn our will and our lives over to the care of God.
—The Third Step

Blessed are those whose strength is in you, who have set their hearts on pilgrimage. They go from strength to strength, till each appears before God in Zion.

—Psalm 84:5, 7

When I cling to God's promises, truly promised by our loving God in the Bible, I feel God's assurance to me of His unfailing love and faithfulness through Jesus Christ my Lord. When my growth through The Twelve Steps seems to go slowly, I thank God for the many promises He has made to me. Through the indwelling Spirit, I go from strength to strength as I pray through the Steps and walk in The Twelve Steps Journey. The Word and Spirit assure me that God will perfect His work in me. Through daily prayer, I have learned to rely only upon God's grace, a grace that He began to work in me even before I began to take the Prayer Steps to Serenity.

God closely connected the Holy Spirit with our prayer life. After I received the Holy Spirit through prayer, I realized that the Spirit life requires a continuous prayer life. If I continually give myself to prayer, then the Spirit can lead me continually. As I submit myself to the Spirit's control, I can avoid destructive behavior and become a true blessing to others.

Am I willing to decide today to turn myself over to the care of God? Am I willing to reaffirm this decision daily—one day at a time? Am I willing to ask God to take control every time I want to follow my feelings and return to my old ways of living? Am I willing to walk on God's road of happiness and peace?

God wants to accomplish a great deal in my life, but my spending time in prayer and fellowship with God is indispensable for God to work fully in my life. Jesus Christ revealed that if I will only open my heart and mouth toward heaven, then He would not fail me or put me to shame but fill me with His love, truth, power, and grace.

To obtain God's blessings, I must pray. I must entirely surrender my heart to God as He has truly revealed himself. I must believe in the power of prayer. I will now rest my weary heart and mind in the assurance that God will care for me and work powerfully in me as I turn my life over to Him, and do so daily in prayer.

Prayer for Today

Dear Father, if I limit you to my finite vision, I am too scared to turn my life over to you. As I pray and read your Word, give me faith to place my life in your hands and rest on your promises. By resting in you and your truths, I can experience the joy and serenity I seek. Today, as I think about my past, I want to turn over to you most especially . . .

Day 19
The Spirit Will Pray for Me

Made a decision to turn our will and our lives over to the care of God.
—The Third Step

In the same way, the Spirit helps us in our weakness. We do not know what we ought to pray for, but the Spirit himself intercedes for us with groans that words cannot express.

—Romans 8:26

If God left me to myself, I would not know how to pray. God stooped down and rescued me in my helplessness by giving me the Holy Spirit to pray for me. The work of the Holy Spirit in the believer's life is deeper than our thoughts or feelings, and God hears the Spirit in our prayers in ways beyond our understanding.

The Holy Spirit teaches what the Bible means about God. The Holy Spirit works in us so we can turn our lives over to God and receive His care. The Holy Spirit helps us humbly admit that any recovery or progress we make is due primarily to God's work in us.

Before I turned my life over to God, He worked upon me from the outside. Now, as a believer, God's Spirit works with power from the inside. From the inside, the Holy Spirit gives me power to change. The Holy Spirit works from the inside out, so others can also enjoy the fruits of my Christ-centered life.

Because I have turned my life over to God, I can come into His presence with the confidence that the Holy Spirit will carry out His work in my prayers. Such confidence will inspire reverence and quietness, and will enable me to depend on the Holy Spirit to present my needs and desires to God in a way that He will accept. Through the Holy Spirit, my prayers will have more value than I can imagine. No wonder the happiness and serenity I feel today is from the Holy Spirit's work in me.

In every prayer of the believer, the Triune God participates. God the Father hears our prayers. We pray in the name of His Son, so He will answer our prayers. And the Holy Spirit prays in us and for us about the things we need. When we turn our lives over to the Triune God, we know that God will hear our prayers and meet our needs. As I pray today and everyday, I will direct my special requests to the Father, the Son, and the Holy Spirit.

Prayer for Today

Dear God, help me to believe in the reality of your Holy Spirit working in my life. Turn my attention from myself, so my heart will make room for your Holy Spirit to indwell me fully. May I come to know your Holy Spirit as the Spirit of Serenity, so I can share your peace with those around me, especially with those who have suffered so much with my weaknesses. Today, so I can turn my life over to your care with greater consistency day by day, turn my obsessive thoughts from . . .

Day 20
Thanking God for His Care

Made a decision to turn our will and our lives over to the care of God.
—The Third Step

And I will pour out on the house of David and the inhabitants of Jerusalem a spirit of grace and supplication. They will look on me, the one they have pierced, and they will mourn for him as one mourns for an only child, and grieve bitterly for him as one grieves for a firstborn son.
—Zechariah 12:10

I thank God for the certain promise that He will care for me now that I have turned my life over to Him. With full assurance of faith, I acknowledge that through the Holy Spirit, God now indwells me as His Temple. God is always present within me and I can rejoice in Him.

The Bible calls the Holy Spirit the "spirit of grace and supplication." The Spirit now lives within me to love and to rule; therefore, I have the power to become a new person. I thank God when I pray, and I ask His

Spirit to fill me with ever more reasons to praise and thank God for His blessings. Thanksgiving in prayer draws my heart closer to God and keeps me consciously aware of His care. The Spirit also dwells within me to teach me how to pray for others in my Fellowship and family as well as myself; these are my prayers of supplication that the Spirit inspires within me.

Without prayer, I found the work of going through The Twelve Steps too hard. At first, I tried to have fellowship with God as I imagined Him to be, but that did not work. When I tried to pray apart from the Holy Spirit's help, I found that communion with God was impossible without the Spirit's praying for me.

The Holy Spirit reveals the Father and the Son to us; and He glorifies the Son. When I turned my life over to the care of Jesus, the Holy Spirit made such changes in me that Jesus received all the praise and thanksgiving for my recovery. The Scriptures reveal that God wants Jesus to receive the glory and honor for our victories. We need to acknowledge Jesus as the Source of our serenity, joy, and eternal happiness.

The Spirit of Holiness teaches me to recognize hatefulness and turn from evil. When I came to understand that the Holy Spirit is the Spirit of Wisdom, Love, and Power, I more readily committed myself to His daily guidance and care through prayer and study of the Scriptures.

Prayer for Today

Dear Father, thank you for the difference I have found in praying with the Holy Spirit, knowing He is the Spirit of Prayer and Serenity. Continue caring for me by helping me to keep changing daily by your power as I pray in Jesus' name and in His Spirit. Today, I especially need your guidance and strength to change . . .

Day 21
The Third Step and the Serenity Prayer

Made a decision to turn our will and our lives over to the care of God.
—The Third Step

*God, grant me the serenity **to accept** the things I cannot change, the courage to change the things I can, and the wisdom to know the difference.*
—The Serenity Prayer

Listen to advice and accept instruction, and in the end you will be wise. Many are the plans in a man's heart, but it is the Lord's purpose that prevails.

—Proverbs 19:20, 21

What stops me from turning my will and my life over to the care of God? Could it be that I still have too much pride, even after I have suffered so much personal pain and have traveled this far in my Prayer Steps to Serenity? Am I too proud to listen to good advice and accept sound instruction? Will I turn my life and future over to the care of God? Through His wise instruction and discipline, God has been trying to bring me back to Him. Now, will I give myself back to God? Many in my Fellowship have discovered that they saved themselves lots of trouble and everlasting suffering when they turned their lives and their will over to the care of God. Will I do that today? Now? This moment?

Ultimately, God's purposes will prevail. If my plans do not succeed, I know that God's plans will; therefore, I pray that God will work out His plans in my life. God will not force His will upon me. The Third Step teaches me that I am the one who can choose or refuse to turn my will and life over to God, the Great Architect of the universe. Do I think that I am smarter than the One Who created all things; or can I believe that the Highest Power in the universe can be trusted to work out all things for my benefit and the happiness and well being of all His creation?

I cannot change God. I cannot make God into someone God is not. What if I did remake God into my own image or according to what I want God to become? What kind of a God would I have? Would I have a god of obsessions, compulsions, and addictions? Would my god become the great enabler of my destructive habits? To find and maintain serenity in this complex and troubled world in which I live, I need to accept the care of the One True God over my life. I need to trust in God's love and care for me daily. I will not even begin to experience lasting serenity until I accept the true God and His care over me.

When I truly pray The Serenity Prayer (and do not simply mouth the words as I hear the prayer recited in my meetings), I make a decision. I ask God for acceptance, change, courage, and the wisdom to live my life on God's terms instead of mine. When I pray The Serenity Prayer, I make a decision to accept the consequences of praying that prayer, of turning my life and will over to the care of God, to have God's purposes established in my life once and for all time. When I pray The Serenity Prayer and walk in the Third Step, I tell God that I want Him to rule over me and overrule any unwise plans I might make, plans that might bring distress or needless suffering to others or me.

When I pray and walk in The Twelve Steps Journey, I know that God will not turn me into a puppet, a mindless automaton, or a robot. Rather, God respects me and the mind and heart He has given me. He will give me instructions in the Bible; give me advice through His faithful followers (who should never contradict the Scriptures in giving guidance, but who may be mistaken sometimes), and give me the leading of the Holy Spirit that He has sent into my heart. God will walk with me through The Twelve Steps as I take each one. God will help me distinguish between His will and my will, so I will not confuse my will with His and turn back to a destructive life of hopelessness. God's will is the door to serenity. Today, I will open that door and take the Third Step over that threshold to lasting joy and peace as I pray.

Prayer for Today

Dear God, as I think about doing what taking this Third Step requires, I confess that in the past I have sometimes felt that you have let me down. I have felt that you have failed me; so it is difficult for me to trust you again. Thank you for being so big, and so big-hearted, that you do not hold this sin and confession against me but truly understand my inmost being. Dear God, as a matter of simple faith, faith in you, faith in this Step, faith in the testimony of others who have taken it successfully, faith that where so many have found recovery and serenity I will find it too, faith in your infallible Word, I take this Step today. I truly pray The Serenity Prayer as I have never prayed it before. And, right now, I turn my life and will over to you and ask you to please care for . . .

Prayer Step Principle

Prayer produces such a change in us as to render it consistent for God to do as it would not be consistent for Him to do otherwise. To pray effectively, you must pray with submission to the will of God.

Charles Finney in *Principles of Prayer*

The Twelve Steps Journey
Step 3 Workbook

Made a decision to turn our will and our lives over to the care of God.
—The Third Step

The LORD their God will care for them; he will restore their fortunes.
—Zephaniah 2:7

Things I have learned about God and prayer:

Things I have learned about myself:

What I have learned about turning my life fully over to the care of God:

What I have learned about others and my relationship with them:

My prayer requests and answers to prayer:

Prayer for Today

God, grant me the Serenity to accept the things I cannot change, the Courage to change the things I can, and the Wisdom to know the difference. Lord God, help me today to . . .

Day 22
The Fourth Step to Serenity

Made a searching and fearless moral inventory of ourselves.
—The Fourth Step

You search out my path and my lying down, and are acquainted with all my ways. Even before a word is on my tongue, O LORD, you know it completely.
—Psalm 139:3, 4

Almost everyone has spent a lot of time hiding from who they really are. In the Fourth Step, I will prayerfully ask God to search out those things in my life that have hurt God, others, and me.

My choices will be moral or immoral depending upon the intention of my heart—the main source of every person's actions. An action that flows from love for God and others is moral—though the right intention does not prevent someone from making a mistake. On the other hand, an action that flows from selfishness and self-centeredness is immoral.

When I take a moral inventory, I will list both the right and wrong things I have said and done, giving scrutiny to my motives. I can thank God for the good things. As I list each action, I need to ask myself, "Why did I do that?" Bill W. often said, "In rationalizing, we often hide a bad intention under a good intention." I need to ask myself, "What is my ultimate intention for everything I do?" I can list helpful things I did from a wrong intention, perhaps things I did to manipulate others. I can list mistakes I made from a good intention, and remind myself not to feel guilty for ignorant mistakes. I bear true guilt for the things I did with a wrong motive.

A moral inventory, or list, needs to include things I have done (both good and bad) and things I have not done (both good and bad); things I could have done and things I should not have done in my life. I can overcome my fears of such a personal searching by reminding myself that I am now under the care of a loving, heavenly Father who will forgive me, give me the courage to face myself, and empower me to change.

In order to be truly complete, I need to include in my list some of the good things that I have done with a good motive. God has given me many gifts and talents. My inventory can also include how I have used some of my time and talents to help others and bring them happiness. When I get discouraged as I make my list, I can look at the good side of my inventory to lift me up and remind me that I am not as totally bad as my efforts to be completely searching have made me appear.

God knows that by my taking a personal inventory of my life I can put myself on the true path to happiness and serenity. I do pray for personal honesty, humility, and sincerity in my attempt to complete my list. I can become the person I truly want to be if I take every Step in this journey.

Prayer for Today

God, grant me the Serenity to accept the things I cannot change, the Courage to change the things I can, and the Wisdom to know the difference. Lord God, help me today to . . .

Day 23
The Root Cause of My Problems

Made a searching and fearless moral inventory of ourselves.
— The Fourth Step

If we claim to be without sin, we deceive ourselves and the truth is not in us.
— 1 John 1:8

I am searching for the root cause of my character defects, and for any reasons within me for my problems. I need to direct my attention first to that, or secondary influences and problems will always plague me and I will never have the healing I seek.

Through prayer and meditation, God will give me proper insight into my true character. God will help me see myself as He sees me and others may see me. I need to stop fooling myself and misleading others. As I begin to list the wrongs I have done, I will overcome the deadness and failure I feel sometimes in my private prayers. As I begin to deal with my problems and their root cause, I will not blame my lack of fellowship with God on Him.

What is the root cause of my problems and my failure to hear from God? Is it selfishness and self-centeredness? "*The Big Book*" says, "Selfishness, self-centeredness! That, we think, is the root of our troubles. Driven by a hundred forms of fear, self-delusion, self-seeking, and self-pity, we step on the toes of our fellows and they retaliate. Sometimes they hurt us, seemingly without provocation, but we invariably find that at some time in the past we have made decisions based on self which later placed us in a position to be hurt." Do most of my shortcomings have their origin in my obsessive self-concern? Have all of my prayers focused on the things I want from God and others? Oh God, help me to recognize this evil and forever renounce it. As "*The Big Book*" warns, "Above everything, we must be rid of this selfishness. We must, or it will kill us! God makes that possible." By your grace, Oh God, help me put you first in my life, and make room in my heart for you and others.

Just two things are possible: walking with the Holy Spirit according to the Scriptures or following my selfish desires and feelings. Oh God, fill me with your Holy Spirit so I will not fulfill the compulsions, unwholesome desires and selfish impulses that harm others or me. Open my mind so I can understand the Scriptures; then, I will know what to do when temptations, compulsions, and unholy desires assault me. Then, I can pray rightly for your Spirit to help me and empower me to do rightly.

Prayer for Today

Oh God, as I begin to list the wrongs I have done, show me their root cause in my self-centeredness. And then, Father, by your grace, help me put the axe to the root of selfishness and remove it completely. Dear Father, fill the hole left in my heart with your love and the personal presence of Jesus Christ. Dear Jesus, make my heart your throne, so selfishness will never take root and grow there again, so your serenity will influence every choice I make and bless every person I meet. Today, show me what I need to change and how I can turn fully to you from . . .

The Fourth Step to
Serenity

Day 24
God Reveals My Problems the Best

Made a searching and fearless moral inventory of ourselves.
—The Fourth Step

But if we walk in the light, as God is in the light, we have fellowship with one another, and the blood of Jesus, his Son, purifies us from all sin.
—1 John 1:7

I need to discover and acknowledge my character defects if I am to understand more fully the grace of God and how His Son can help me. As I prayerfully read the Bible, the Holy Spirit will shine His light, give me understanding, and apply God's Word to the defects in my life. My God-given conscience will help me in this task, either commending or condemning my behavior. The Bible will teach me how horrible my sins and their consequences are. These truths will motivate me to avoid sin. Daily, prayerful reading and asking God to point out my sins in the light of His Word takes courage that only the Holy Spirit can give me.

I thank God that the Holy Spirit will not show me all of my defects all at once. God will gently and lovingly show me only what He knows I can bear and deal with at the moment that day. Over time, God will help me remove, or He will remove, each defect. Thankfully, just listing my defects is not the final Step in The Twelve Steps Journey.

If others try to be the Holy Spirit for me, and take my moral inventory by pointing out all of my defects, the pain and shame of admitting my character defects may be more than I can bear. If I try to take the moral inventory of others, I may influence them to avoid their pain and run away from their problems, remain in denial, or return to their destructive behaviors. With good reasons Jesus asked His followers, "Why do you look at the speck of sawdust in your brother's eye and pay no attention to the plank in your own eye? How can you say to your brother, 'Brother, let me take the speck out of your eye,' when you yourself fail to see the plank in your own eye? You hypocrite, first take the plank out of your eye, and then you will see clearly to remove the speck from your brother's eye" (Luke 6:41-42). Taking my own moral inventory is a big enough Step for me to take in my recovery without taking the inventory of others too.

I am prayerfully working through the Fourth Step so God can gently show me my problems and give me His remedy. I cannot allow myself to think that daily sin, selfishness, and self-seeking are impossible to overcome and cease to mourn over my sinfulness. I will make spiritual progress and find true happiness only if I bring my actions before my conscious mind, evaluate them, and confess every transgression against God, others and myself. Only by confessing my faults to God will I begin to experience the freedom and serenity He intends for me to enjoy each day.

Prayer for Today

Dear God, make my conscience tender. If I sin, break my heart and rob me of my serenity. When I am tempted, bring my conscience to bear down upon me with its solemn warnings, so I will not sin against you, others, or myself. As I read your Word, write your Law of Love on my heart, and give me the power to overcome my defects and do right. Help me overcome my fear of taking my own moral inventory, and remind me that taking this Step is the only way to lasting joy and peace. Today, show me that I need to acknowledge, and help me take responsibility for the faults of...

Day 25
The Problem of Prayerlessness

Made a searching and fearless moral inventory of ourselves.
—The Fourth Step

As for me, far be it from me that I should sin against the Lord by failing to pray for you.
—1 Samuel 12:23

The sin of prayerlessness can bring about terrible effects. In saying my prayers, I can actually not be praying at all, because my "praying" may be just giving God my list of selfish desires and making selfish demands that I want God to fulfill as soon as possible. If I deceive myself and do not get better or experience the serenity I seek, I can begin to distrust God and prayer, when it is my way of not really praying that is my problem. Prayerlessness can be a hasty and superficial communion with God, a hurrying to get on with "more important things," a way of telling God that He is not really all that important to me.

Just "saying" my prayers everyday will not help me hate sin or give me the power to flee from temptations. Praying needs to be more than just saying words, the same words, over and over again. Just praying The Serenity Prayer repeatedly without meaning every word can be a sign of prayerlessness. True praying and a meaningful Quiet Time can result in a joyful fellowship with God and a time of resting in the presence of God.

As God's child, I am slowly learning more about prayer, and that nothing but hidden, humble, constant fellowship with God can teach me to hate sin, as God wants me to hate it. As I open my hidden life to God, He will help me hate sin and give me the hope of overcoming my flaws. Only by maintaining a constant nearness to the living Lord Jesus will He give me unceasing power to understand how to detest and conquer my character defects and weaknesses.

As God's Word and Spirit reveal my sins to me, I need to develop a deeper understanding of prayer and God's willingness to grant me pardon. As I look to Jesus and remember what it cost Him to forgive, purify, and renew me, He gives me power and works out the victory over temptation that would destroy my peace with God and others. He fills me with peace, the real peace of God within me; and He gives me joy, a joy that overflows into the lives of others.

I can never repay the Lord Jesus for His gifts of love to me, but I can linger longer in His presence and express my love and gratitude with words of praise. As I praise and thank Him, I will become more like Him, and His holiness will rest upon me.

Prayer for Today

Dear Father, as I list my flaws, help me see that these led Jesus to die on the cross for me. He gave up a serene life on earth and embraced the suffering of the cross for me. He rose from the dead to give me eternal life and daily strength. In the days ahead, help me to spend more time with you as I pray longer over your Word. Grant me the serenity that comes only from consciously living in your presence. Today, I pray for the Holy Spirit to search my heart so I can list the errors of my ways, and as I list them, I want to praise you for . . .

Day 26
The One Who Can Save Me

Made a searching and fearless moral inventory of ourselves.
—The Fourth Step

She will give birth to a son, and you are to give him the name Jesus, because he will save his people from their sins.
—Matthew 1:21

As I list the things I have done to harm others and myself, I need to remember that the Lord Jesus will forgive me and save me from my transgressions. The name Jesus means Savior. He came to save me here, now, and forever.

As His follower, Jesus wants me to love and adore Him each day. Have I done this? If not, have I put this on my list? Does my inventory include the times I have honored and dishonored God?

Through daily communion with Jesus, He will save me from my sins. He will reveal himself to me, and through the power of His love, He will cast out my love for sin. He will save me from my trespasses by the power of a daily personal fellowship with Him.

To be saved from my sins, I need to bring my heart to Jesus, even with the sin that is in it, and ask Him to be my almighty personal Savior. He can save me from every sin in my moral inventory. As Jesus and I spend more time together and express our mutual love for one another, by the work of His Holy Spirit in my heart, His love will expel and conquer all sin within me.

I need to learn the blessedness of maintaining fellowship with Jesus each day. Communion with Jesus is the secret of all true happiness and holiness. As I do this more and more, my heart will long for the hour of prayer, because it will be the best hour of the day. Through prayer and the grace He pours out upon me, every day of my life will honor Him, and someday He will honor me in the presence of the holy angels.

As I spend time alone with Jesus, I will experience His presence enabling me to love Him, serve Him, and walk in His ways. Through unbroken fellowship with a holy God, I will have the secret power of a truly holy and happy life.

Prayer for Today

Dear Father, I find listing my sins one-by-one to be heart rending, but as I do so I remember that you will forgive me for each sin. You can expel my love for any sin and help me conquer my addictions. Please give me the faith I need today to keep on working this Step, knowing that serenity will be the fruit. Today, please reveal to me by your Spirit the wrongs in my life that I still fail to recognize; and as you show them to me one-by-one please save me from . . .

Day 27
My Reason for Rejoicing

Made a searching and fearless moral inventory of ourselves.
—The Fourth Step

Jesus said, "Father, forgive them, for they do not know what they are doing." And they divided up his clothes by casting lots.
—Luke 23:34

As I continue working on my moral inventory, I rejoice that God loves me in spite of what I have done. God loves His enemies as well as His friends. Just as Jesus prayed for His enemies, as He hung on the cross and they cast lots for his clothes as they mocked Him, I know He is praying for me as I make a list of the wrongs I have done. He died for me, and now from heaven He intercedes for me with rejoicing as I complete this Step.

Jesus calls me to love my enemies too, to pray for them and bless them. As I think of those who influenced me to believe falsehoods and do wrong, I am tempted to hold a grudge against them or even hate them. As I think about these people, I need to forgive them just as Jesus forgives me. Hanging on to old resentments will only hinder my spiritual growth and keep me from having the close communion with God that I need through prayer.

When I think of the repentant thief who prayed to Jesus for mercy as he hung upon the cross beside Him, I marvel at the wonderful love of God. I rejoice in Jesus' readiness to forgive and the joy He must have felt when He said, "I tell you the truth, today you will be with me in paradise" (Luke 23:43). I trust in God's ready forgiveness, and this faith inspires me to keep on examining my life thoroughly.

The cross of Jesus is a cross of love. I owe my future to the sacrificial, redeeming love of God. As they nailed Jesus' hands to the cross, He was reaching out to the world with love. When He rose from the dead, His freed arms embraced the world with love. Will I let Him embrace me? Will I run to Him so He can enfold me in His arms? As I pray to God and confess my errors and trespasses, I know that because He loves me that He will forgive me and enable me to follow Him more nearly each day.

Prayer for Today

Dear Jesus, the only thought that sustains me, as I look at my life with all the degrading things that I have done, is the certain knowledge of your love and willingness to forgive me, accept me, and give me a new life on earth and in heaven. Thank you for dying to make my forgiveness possible and to grant me everlasting joy and serenity. Today, reveal to me the sins of omission in my life. As I begin to listen quietly, speak to my heart so I can list . . .

Day 28
The Fourth Step and the Serenity Prayer

Made a searching and fearless moral inventory of ourselves.
—The Fourth Step

*God, grant me the serenity to accept **the things** I cannot change, the courage to change the things I can, and the wisdom to know the difference.*
—The Serenity Prayer

Many times God delivered them, but they were bent on rebellion and they wasted away in their sin. But God took note of their distress when he heard their cry.
—Psalm 106:43, 44

When we took the Fourth Step the first time, most of us did not know that we needed to list both our good character traits as well as our bad character traits. Some of us were too low at the time to even think anything good about ourselves. If anything, our list on the good side would have been almighty short. Moreover, rather than thinking about our character traits, most of us thought only of the bad deeds we had done, and did not consider how these had led to the formation of our character, deep seated resentments, and irrational fears. Still, God honored our honest efforts and granted us the joy and serenity that comes from completing an inventory of ourselves.

As we pray The Serenity Prayer, we come to accept "the things" we cannot change. The more we work the Program, the more we understand that "the things" are real; just as real as a sofa, table, or vase of lovely roses. The unwise things we said and did in the past had real and lasting consequences, and they have stayed with us and others far longer than many of the material things we have owned. The hurtful things that others said or did to us, even as children, have lasted far longer than the box of crayons and pencils we took on the first day of school. Sometimes, "the things" have led us to resent others and others to resent us. We need to list all "the things" in our moral inventory, and remember that many of these things have had lasting consequences in our lives and in the lives of others. As we list "the things" in our moral inventory, the good and the bad, we can say The Serenity Prayer every time we relive the pain and shame of the past and feel as though we cannot finish this Step: "God, grant me the serenity to accept *the things*." He will answer this prayer! He will give us the courage and strength to complete our task.

As we create our moral inventory, we list "the things" in writing, just as we might take a business inventory at the end of each year (and some in recovery take a new moral inventory at the close of each year). In addition to listing some of the good things we have done along with the bad, we can also list some of the things we lack. Before baking a cake, a cook will often check to see if they have all of the ingredients and enough of each one. Likewise, our moral inventory can list "the things" we lack: lack of love, lack of contact with God, lack of faith, lack of healthy relationships, lack of self-control, lack of wisdom in making decisions, lack of persistence, lack of self-confidence or God-confidence. What we lack are also some of "the things" we need and "the things" we need on our list.

In taking the Fourth Step, we do not need to think ahead of ourselves. We do not need to fear taking the Fifth Step as we are taking the Fourth Step. We do not need to think about how to forgive others. We do not need to spend time trying to figure out how to overcome our resentments or resenting the need to overcome our resentments. We do not need to find out the root cause of "the things." We do not need to try to fix blame on others or ourselves. We just make a list. God will help us do all of the necessary things when the time is right, and He will do so in ways that cast out our fears, give us serenity, and fill our hearts with true happiness. He will do so in ways that give us the release and true recovery we seek.

The Bible gives us a reliable record of God's performance, and when people in trouble called out to Him the Bible says, "God delivered them." Likewise, God will deliver us no matter what we have done or failed to do in the past. As we follow the Prayer Steps to Serenity, God will give us all we need for substantial wholeness in this life. As we take our moral inventory, we can do so while constantly calling out to God, trusting that He will deliver us and enable us to complete The Twelve Steps Journey.

As we neared the completion of our moral inventory, we recognized with deep agony of spirit that we had been bent on rebellion for many years. In rebelling against God, we rebelled against commonsense. We rebelled against ourselves and those who tried to help us. Our rebellion led to the state in which we found ourselves. We could identify with those the Bible speaks of when it says, "they wasted away in their sin." But thankfully, this was not the final word! When we called out to God in our misery, when God heard our cry, we found that God took note of our distress. God loved us in spite of ourselves and our rebellion. God loved us in spite of our moral inventory. When we cried out to God and He saw our serious plight and sincere prayer, He took note and led us to the Person and Program that met our needs. When we saw that God loved us enough to send His Son to die and rise again for us, we knew that He would give us a meaningful recovery and the everlasting joy we needed through faith in Jesus.

Prayer for Today

Dear God, as I think about what the Fourth Step requires, help me to not look too far beyond this Step. Show me if I need to learn more before I make my inventory list, but please help me avoid procrastination. As I continue to pray through these Steps, help me to focus intently on completing this Step. Today, I pray that you will encourage me by forgiving me and giving me serenity in spite of my having…

Prayer Step Principle

Sincerity in prayer motivates your heart to condemn your sin plainly, without concealing the facts, intentions or feelings under false excuses and pretences. When we pray from the heart, we cry to God heartily without complimenting ourselves or praising our righteousness.

John Bunyan in *How to Pray in the Spirit*

The Twelve Steps Journey
Step 4 Workbook

Made a searching and fearless moral inventory of ourselves.
—The Fourth Step

I the LORD search the heart and examine the mind, to reward a man according to his conduct, according to what his deeds deserve.
—Jeremiah 17:10

Things I have learned about God and prayer:

Things I have learned about myself:

What I have learned about the worst sins in my past:

What I have learned about others and my relationship with them:

My prayer requests and answers to prayer:

Prayer for Today

God, grant me the Serenity to accept the things I cannot change, the Courage to change the things I can, and the Wisdom to know the difference. Lord God, help me today to . . .

Day 29
The Fifth Step to Serenity

Admitted to God, to ourselves and to another human being the exact nature of our wrongs.

—The Fifth Step

I confess my iniquity; I am troubled by my sin.

—Psalm 38:18

As we evaluate and admit our wrongs, we need to think about what influenced us to do those things. We need to examine the "*exact nature* of our wrongs." Did our family background or some disappointing experience influence us to take the path that led to our actions and addictions? Can we acknowledge these influences and at the same time accept the full responsibility for our past decisions and deeds? Can we remember the turning points or crossroads when we deliberately made wrong choices—even if partially from ignorance?

Those who create temptations intend for their products or services to be addicting. If they were not addicting, and creating a demand, how could anyone successfully advertise and sell such harmful indulgences? Taking even one forbidden action can lead to bad habits. Each wrong choice makes it harder to say "no" to the next temptation. Thoughts and actions lead to habits that form our character. Admitting my responsibility for the exact nature of my wrongs will lead to my spiritual, mental, and physical healing, and the formation of the honorable character I seek

As I take the Fifth Step, I need to remember that God's loving presence is with me. He enfolds me with loving arms and holds me so close that nothing I confess would ever influence Him to let me go. As I confess to God, He understands, forgives and consoles me, as I have never been understood, forgiven and consoled before. As I confess each trespass, His Spirit will heal my breaking and repentant heart. Because He once lived upon this earth, Jesus understands everything I have ever done and will forgive everything I confess.

Through prayer, God can lead me to someone with the compassion of Jesus to hear my confessions. As "*The Big Book*" reminds me, "Those of us belonging to a religious denomination which requires confession must, and of course, will want to go to the properly appointed authority whose duty it is to receive it. Though we have no religious conception, we may still do well to talk with someone ordained by an established religion. We often find such a person quick to see and understand our problem." He will forgive me too, so I can confess my defects humbly, honestly, and without fear. When I take my Fifth Step, my Sponsor and I can pray for the healing and strength that I need to complete the Program. As I tell him or her my life story, I will experience the housecleaning I need to overcome my weaknesses. Taking my Fifth Step can also free me from the fear and tension that rob me of my serenity and lead me back into the delusional thinking that my addictions, compulsions, and dependencies are not killing me.

Prayer for Today

God, grant me the Serenity to accept the things I cannot change, the Courage to change the things I can, and the Wisdom to know the difference. Lord God, help me today to . . .

Day 30
Conscience and Confession

Admitted to God, to ourselves and to another human being the exact nature of our wrongs.

—The Fifth Step

If we confess our sins, he is faithful and just and will forgive us our sins and purify us from all unrighteousness.

—1 John 1:9

For my conscience to work as God intended, I must truly repent of the wrongs I have done. I must confess my outward actions (that I and others may know about) and the hidden thoughts that have prompted me to act in ways that were harmful. I need to consider what might have motivated me to do wrong. To find happiness and wholeness, to find freedom from the power of my blighted past, I must list and confess each individual sin and shortcoming by name. I must be intensely personal as I pray to God and ask for His help and forgiveness.

How wonderful to think that a holy God invites me, an unworthy sinner, to come to Him for the assurance of forgiveness and fellowship. He invites me to come and experience the depth of companionship with Him that only the forgiven enjoy. He created me in His image and redeemed me by His Son so I can have salvation from the power of sin and life everlasting. How wonderful to realize that God has provided the solution to my every problem. Surely, God does not want any sin that I have failed to confess to stand in the way of a blessed and glorious relationship with Him. With the help of God's Spirit, the Program helps me solve the problem of sin.

When I am sick, I try to discover the true cause of my illness and the best way to treat it. With some illnesses, I need a doctor to diagnose my problem and give me the treatment I need. When I confess my trespasses to a trustworthy person, he can give me the treatment I need: the assurance of forgiveness and restoration. This is always one of the most important steps toward recovery and lasting serenity. The cause of many of my problems is the burden of the sins that I carry and have not confessed. After I take the time to confess every sin, God has promised to forgive me and cleanse me from all my corruptions. Then I will know that the smiling face of God is upon me when I pray.

Prayer for Today

Dear Father, as I confess my sins and shortcomings, my defects of character and the harm these have caused, show me everything that I must confess—when you have made me ready to remember them. Show me the gravity of my transgressions slowly; otherwise, I could not take the pain and keep on taking this Step. Restore my serenity and cleanse me from my sins as I confess them, so I can know the joys of completing this Step as I go along. Today, you have reminded me of some trespasses that I have suppressed and not confessed, so I want to confess now and receive your forgiveness for the trespasses of . . .

Day 31
Life Follows Death to Self

Admitted to God, to ourselves and to another human being the exact nature of our wrongs.

—The Fifth Step

I tell you the truth, unless a kernel of wheat falls to the ground and dies, it remains only a single seed. But if it dies, it produces many seeds.

—John 12:24

Every seed teaches how I will receive a beautiful and bountiful life by dying to self. Confession kills pride and brings forth the beautiful fruit of humility. God gives grace to the humble. Jesus had to pass through death in all its bitterness and suffering before He could rise to heaven and impart His life to those He redeemed. I must learn the lesson of self-sacrifice. I must die to the selfish and self-centered life, which is the nature and root cause of all my wrongs. Jesus can help me turn from self-centeredness to a sacrificial life of God-centeredness.

When I admit my shortcomings to God and another human being, I die inside. However, the death of pride will lead me to new life, peace of mind, and the assurance of God's accepting and forgiving love.

I once wondered, "Did Jesus Christ really need to die?" I do not understand it all, but God laid upon Him the evil deeds of us all, and Jesus yielded to the Father so through His death we might have life. Jesus' death made our forgiveness and new life possible.

As I confess my inner bondage to many evil things, through my fellowship with Christ and His cross I will die to my preoccupation with self and He will free me to live for God and others. My prayers will become God-centered instead of self-centered. With joy and eagerness, I will learn to obey His call to bear my cross and die daily. In every prayer, I will see myself as "crucified with Christ." Knowing that Jesus works within me will inspire me to die daily and gladly the death to self that will bring me into fellowship with Him and give me new life.

The Spirit of Christ Jesus, the Risen Lord, can make His death and life my daily experience. In yielding submissive prayer, Jesus will give me power to overcome temptation and conquer every spiritual enemy.

Prayer for Today

Dear Jesus, how humiliating to think of confessing my sins to you and another human being, and yet many in my Fellowship have told of the joy of sins forgiven and the new life they received from the confession of their faith and faults. Give me courage to do what seems impossible to me now, and remind me that I am on the path of serenity. By your Spirit, speak to my conscience and show me if I have any self-centered habits that I need to reject and confess. Today, even now, I confess that you have shown me the faults of . . .

The Fifth Step to Serenity

Day 32
God's Forgiveness Inspires My Love

Admitted to God, to ourselves and to another human being the exact nature of our wrongs.

—The Fifth Step

The LORD, the LORD, the compassionate and gracious God, slow to anger, abounding in love and faithfulness, maintaining love to thousands, and forgiving wickedness, rebellion and sin.

—Exodus 34:6, 7

Until a person really confesses his sins to God, he cannot understand how abundantly God forgives. Through confessing my sins, I will come to know by experience the riches of God's mercy. By His faithfulness and abounding love, God has led me to the point of being ready to admit to Him the exact nature of my wrongs. I cannot doubt that His compassion and grace are also able to forgive me and restore me to fellowship with Him. Confession will remove all the barriers between God and me, and my prayers will be completely unhindered. True confession leads to true communion and fellowship with God.

Through understanding more of God's character, through seeing His hatred of sin and His love for people, through contemplating the amazing fact that He is holy yet slow to anger, I will come to love Him more. The secret of maintaining the openness with God that I seek is being willing to confess any sins I commit each day. As I confess my shortcomings and seek His cleansing from all unrighteousness, I will keep my heart and mind clean, and I will refuse to allow impure thoughts and images to enter my mind. His Spirit will help me keep this resolve. As I meet with God each day, I will live in the light of His love. I have learned the secret of success in prayer: I need to draw near to God with absolute surrender to His will and desire to know and walk in His ways each day.

When I know with assurance that God forgives, and will forgive me when I admit my wrongs, I can approach the Throne of Grace with boldness. Completing the Fifth Step will go a long way in helping me learn more about effective prayer—prayer that receives the answer it seeks.

Prayer for Today

Dear Father in heaven, I once continually disobeyed your command to love you, but when you reached out to me in the love of Jesus and forgave me, when you opened the way for me to come into your presence, when you gave me serenity, I fell in love with you. Fill me with your loving presence and do not let me go, so my love for you will grow each day. I confess and ask you to forgive me for the times I know you were reaching out to me in love and I selfishly turned to my own way. Today, I specifically ask you to forgive me for...

Day 33
God Will Forgive My Prayerlessness

Admitted to God, to ourselves and to another human being the exact nature of our wrongs.

—The Fifth Step

But when you pray, go into your room, close the door and pray to your Father, who is unseen. Then your Father, who sees what is done in secret, will reward you.

—Matthew 6:6

No one other than God and the one who helps me take my Fifth Step need know the exact nature of my wrongs. But after I take the Fifth Step in secret, I will have the freeness and openness I have needed to pray to God in secret. As I spend more and more time with God, He will make such a difference in my life that others will openly see the rewards of walking The Twelve Steps Journey and doing so in constant prayer and reliance on God.

The Lord Jesus, the one who saves us from our sins, is able and willing to deliver me from all sin. By trusting more in Him, He will deliver me from the sin of prayerlessness and failing to spend time with Him in secret prayer. To experience His deliverance, I must acknowledge and confess in a childlike and simple way my sin of not using a private place of prayer and spending a Quiet Time with God. Almost all of my problems have come from my failing to spend time with God and asking God to lead me, free me from evil, and empower me to do good. With deep sorrow and shame, I need to confess my failure to spend quality time with God in prayer and meditation upon His Word.

I need to confess that I was deceived in thinking that I could solve my problems and get through life in my own strength, apart from the Bible's teachings and God's power to do His will. I need to confess that I thought I could pray as I ought to pray without needing any help from the Holy Spirit. I need to confess that the power of the world and my self-confidence led me astray and that I do not have the strength to do better alone.

If I will confess these things with all my heart, God will give me wonderful success as I continue stepping out in faith in the Prayer Steps to Serenity. As I confess my wrongdoings to God and another person, God will free me from the power of sin and give me the serenity upon which my recovery depends.

Prayer for Today

O God, lead me to a person who will understand these things as I confess the great sin of not spending time in secret prayer with you. I pray that you will reveal to me the name of the person I am to consult when I take my Fifth Step and confess all my wrongs. Please, O Lord, do not allow my time of confession to destroy my serenity, but give me your peace as I confess my shortcomings. Today, I ask that you will bring to my mind the names of those people who may help me with this Step, people such as . . .

Day 34
My Forgiveness Brings Singing

Admitted to God, to ourselves and to another human being the exact nature of our wrongs.

—The Fifth Step

I acknowledged my sin to you and did not cover up my iniquity. I said, "I will confess my transgressions to the Lord"—and you forgave the guilt of my sin.

—Psalm 32:5

Confession can be superficial. Honest confession gives power over sin. In fellowship with the Lord Jesus, I need to confess every sin with an open and sincere heart, for every sin will hinder victorious faith and living.

Once, King David was unwilling to confess his sins, but then he learned: "When I kept silent, my bones wasted away through my groaning all day long. For day and night, your hand was heavy upon me; my strength was sapped as in the heat of summer. Then I acknowledged my sin to you and did not cover up my iniquity. I said, 'I will confess my transgressions to the LORD'—and you forgave the guilt of my sin" (Psalm 32:3-5). He also discovered that after confession God surrounded him with "songs of deliverance" (Psalm 32:7).

When God chastens or disciplines me, He does so to save me from sin, now and forever. When I return to God and confess, all heaven rejoices. Jesus declared, "I tell you, there is rejoicing in the presence of the angels of God over one sinner who repents" (Luke 15:10). Furthermore, "I tell you that in the same way there is more rejoicing in heaven over one sinner who repents than over ninety-nine righteous persons who do not need to repent" (Luke 15:7). I must not neglect to take this Step in prayer!

When I confess my sin with shame, I also hand it over to God. I trust God to take it away. Taking the Fifth Step reminds me that I am unable to rid myself of my guilt by myself. I must act in faith that God will deliver me through the precious promises Jesus has made to those who repent.

As I work through The Twelve Steps Journey, I will discover two truths by experience. First, I will know that God has forgiven me for my sins. Second, I will learn that Jesus is cleansing me from my sins and keeping me from falling into bondage again. As I seek prayer fellowship with Jesus each day, I need not fear confessing each sin in the confident assurance that He will forgive and deliver me. God never fails to keep His promises.

Prayer for Today

Dear Jesus, I know you save your people from their sins. I believe in the great power for living that I will find through confessing my sins, because you have borne the great burden of my sin and guilt. Thank you for being both my Lord and Savior, today and forever. Thank you for helping me experience eternal life today and the serenity that comes from your presence within my heart. Today, I want to praise you and thank you again, especially for . . .

Day 35
The Fifth Step and the Serenity Prayer

Admitted to God, to ourselves and to another human being the exact nature of our wrongs.

—The Fifth Step

*God, grant me the serenity to accept the things **I cannot change**, the courage to change the things I can, and the wisdom to know the difference.*

—The Serenity Prayer

Praise the Lord, O my soul, and forget not all his benefits—who forgives all your sins and heals all your diseases, who redeems your life from the pit and crowns you will love and compassion, who satisfies your desires with good things so that your youth is renewed like the eagle's.

— Psalm 103:2-5

The things "I cannot change," which I pray about daily in The Serenity Prayer, are precisely those things I have listed in my moral inventory in Step Four and confess in Step Five. As I take the Fifth Step with God and a trusted Counselor or Sponsor in the Program, I do so with The Serenity Prayer foremost in my heart and mind. Praying The Serenity Prayer enables me to keep in contact with God and receive His loving Spirit of forgiveness as I admit to Him and another human being the exact nature of my wrongs—the things "I cannot change."

I need to remember that I cannot go back in time and make things different, as much as I might want to in order to remove my regrets. These are things I cannot change, but these are precisely the things that God will forgive and others may also forgive by His grace. God can enable me to have a relationship with Him and others that is unhindered by the things I have done in the past and the regrets I feel today.

As I talk to God and another person about my wrongs, God will not change history any more than the person I admit my wrongs to has the power to change history. But I have learned that God's loving mercy will help me change my attitude toward the past and the people I have wronged (and who have wronged me). Changing my attitude, granting me the assurance of forgiveness, filling me with His Spirit of love, mercy, forgiveness, and power will give me the serenity and ability I need to face tomorrow and everyday—one day at a time.

On the day I take my Fifth Step, I can praise the Lord for the benefits He has given me personally, through this Program, and in my Fellowship. He promises me in the Bible that He will not only forgive me but also heal all my diseases. The disease of resentment, the disease of addiction, compulsion, co-dependency, and other illnesses can all be healed by God. Some of my diseases He will heal in this life; other diseases He will heal in the life to come. Some of the consequences of my behavior in the past "I cannot change," but God can. He can and will give me substantial healing in many areas of my life as I practice the Prayer Steps to Serenity and trust in Him and His Word.

I have heard some say as they reflect on the almost universal experience of those working the Program, "I was so far down that all I could do was look up." God has promised to redeem our life from the pit, and the testimony of most in the Program is that God did that for them. If life is ever "the pits," the good news of God includes His desire and ability to lift us out of "the pits" and give us courage, wisdom, and power to change.

Why does God do so much for us when we complete the Fifth Step? Not because we have earned His favor as we take the Step, but because God is the God of love and compassion. Moreover, after we begin practicing the Prayer Steps to Serenity, we can go into the presence of God wearing the crowns He has placed upon our heads. We cannot see these crowns physically, for they are the crowns of love and compassion—the very character of God himself that He bestows upon us when He pours His Spirit into our lives. By His Spirit working in us, others will be able to experience personally the changes that wearing these crowns make in us. Eventually, many of the good desires we felt when we entered the Program will be given to us by God himself, and He will return a measure of our unspoiled youth to us.

Prayer for Today

Dear God, as I think about what the Fifth Step requires, help me to trust fully in you and your wonderful promises to me. Help me to find just the right person, the person of your choice, who will hear me take Step Five. Prepare us both, mentally, spiritually, and emotionally to deal with all of the issues on my list that we must discuss. Give them the courage and the wisdom to share with me what I need to hear as I complete this Step. Open my heart and mind to receive the truths that you have revealed to them to share with me. Today, help me face and resolve in my heart and mind the one big thing, or things, that may be keeping me from taking this Step. Grant me peace that passes understanding as you and I prayerfully discuss my problems with ...

Prayer Step Principle

Prayer, to be effectual, must be offered from right motives. Prayer should not be selfish, but should be dictated by a supreme regard for the glory of God. A great deal of prayer is offered from pure selfishness.

Charles Finney in *Principles of Prayer*

The Twelve Steps Journey
Step 5 Workbook

Admitted to God, to ourselves and to another human being the exact nature of our wrongs.

—The Fifth Step

He is able to deal gently with those who are ignorant and are going astray, since he himself is subject to weakness.

—Hebrews 5:2

Things I have learned about God and prayer:

Things I have learned about myself:

What I have learned about the power of confession and forgiveness:

What I have learned about others and my relationship with them:

My prayer requests and answers to prayer:

Prayer for Today

God, grant me the Serenity to accept the things I cannot change, the Courage to change the things I can, and the Wisdom to know the difference. Lord God, help me today to . . .

Day 36
The Sixth Step to Serenity

Were entirely ready to have God remove all these defects of character.
—The Sixth Step

Wash away all my iniquity and cleanse me from all my sin. For I know my transgressions, and my sin is always before me. Restore to me the joy of your salvation and grant me a willing spirit to sustain me.
—Psalm 51:2, 3, 12

How wonderful to have The Twelve Steps to follow in just the right order! As I examined my life in the Fourth Step, I could be honest with myself and not worry about the future or about what I would do with what I discovered. And then, after making my moral inventory, I began to concentrate on finding the right person with whom I would share my grief and guilt. After taking the Fifth Step, I felt such peace and release that I could look with real hope to the future and begin to think seriously about what actions I would take regarding my defects of character.

As I think about my addictions, cravings, and weaknesses, I know I want these removed. I know how destructive they have been. As I think about my compulsive behaviors, I know I do not want to be a slave to these any longer. However, as I think about some of my dependencies, I am so comfortable in some that I wonder if I truly want to give them up. And yet, if I am to be whole and maintain my serenity, then unhealthy dependent relationships with substances or people need to be changed. I need to pray for God to make me ready and give me the strength to have these addictions and dependencies transformed into new relationships and destructive ones removed.

I also need to get rid of all the bad habits I cling to, habits that will eventually destroy my body and mind, even if I do rationalize that they are helping me cope right now with my feelings. Am I entirely ready to give up all my bad habits? With God's help, I can and I will.

I will pray for God to strengthen my will, so I will make a firm decision to have all these defects of character removed. Each Step I have taken has required me to make a decision and take action. Every Step has required me to make some sacrifice; yet, with each self-sacrifice I have gained more than I have given up. I know that God has been with me empowering me to make these decisions and take every action. I praise God for how far I have come in my recovery! I know that He will go with me each step of the way as I continue to pray through and work through the Prayer Steps to Serenity—one day at a time—sometimes moment by moment.

After I take Step Six, I will have walked through half of The Twelve Steps Journey. As I look at the progress I have made, I know that with God's help I can work through all the Prayer Steps—one day at a time. I need to keep reminding myself over and over again, that with God's help I can achieve the success I seek and find reasons for rejoicing each day. Always, just one day at a time.

Prayer for Today

God, grant me the Serenity to accept the things I cannot change, the Courage to change the things I can, and the Wisdom to know the difference. Lord God, help me today to . . .

The Sixth Step to Serenity

Day 37
God Will Remove My Fear

Were entirely ready to have God remove all these defects of character.
—The Sixth Step

Being delivered out of the hands of our enemies, we should serve Him without fear, in holiness and righteousness, before Him, all our days.
—Luke 1:74, 75

I am my own greatest enemy. My own character defects and shortcomings can cause me far greater harm than anyone else can. But these need not ruin the rest of my life. God can remove them, and then fill the vacancies they leave with His holy presence, love, and eternal joy. But am I ready to have God remove my defects of character? Or, do I want to live with the continual fear that my actions may someday destroy me and others?

If I humbly bow before the Lord Jesus, and ask Him to rule in my life, then He will remove all my shortcomings and fill me with His loving presence. Thank God for His promise that Jesus will live His life of loving power in me. O God, help me know by experience this fact of His presence in my life each day.

Through the Holy Spirit, Jesus will dwell in me and give me the power to keep from doing evil. Through Jesus abiding in me, I will have the desire and the power to do God's will in all things. Think of the inspired words of Zacharias quoted above, as he prophesied the deliverance that the Lord Jesus would bring. As we serve Him, we have no reason to fear Him. These are the words of God, and they show what He will do for those who seek Him and desire to serve Him.

God's promises are sure, and He fulfills them in those who wholeheartedly and confidently claim them. Claim this promise for yourself today: "I will sprinkle clean water on you, and you will be clean; I will cleanse you from all your impurities and from all your idols. And I will put my Spirit in you and move you to follow my decrees and be careful to keep my laws. I the LORD have spoken, and I will do it (Ezekiel 36:25, 27, 36b). O God, I pray that I will know the cleansing power of Jesus Christ in my heart, and I ask that my living a clean life for Him will bring abundant blessings to others and me.

Prayer for Today

Lord Jesus, help me to see deeply into my heart and admit that apart from you I can do nothing. Help me see you as you really are, and my defects as they really are. Help me to become entirely ready to have all my character defects removed so lasting serenity can be restored. Help me cast off my favorite vices, so I can be substantially whole and receive your promised presence. Today, I pray that you will encourage me and help me become willing to remove this major defect and weakness that I bring before you now in prayer, confession, and repentance for . . .

The Sixth Step to Serenity

Day 38
Jesus Promises to Transform Me

Were entirely ready to have God remove all these defects of character.
—The Sixth Step

I will do whatever you ask in my name, so that the Son may bring glory to the Father.

—John 14:13

When I receive Jesus as my Lord and Savior, God will grant me all the fullness of His redeeming grace and presence. Through fellowship with Jesus, I will enjoy redemption day by day. By maintaining a close, daily fellowship with Jesus, He will keep me from slipping back into my old ways. He makes it possible for me to persevere in a living, powerful, prayerful, life of obedience that gives me peace with God and makes peace with others possible.

In Jesus, God promises to remove all my defects of character, but I must become ready for Him to remove them and ask Him to do so. In my morning prayers, I can begin an intimate, spiritual, personal and uninterrupted relationship with my Lord throughout the day. In answer to my prayers, He will manifest himself with great power in my life. In the Lord Jesus, all the attributes of God will work powerfully within me and morally transform me. When I ask Jesus to remove my character defects, He will do it. Daily fellowship with Him in prayer will give me the power I need to overcome every temptation to return to my old destructive ways.

As the glorified Son of God, Jesus' presence can fill me at all times and give me the power I need to live a transformed life. As a disciple of Jesus, I need to learn this lesson: Jesus loves me so much that He wants me near Him without a break so I can experience His love. Every time I feel powerless to change, I need to remind myself of His ever-present love for me and of His desire to work His life-transforming power within me. Remembering this will give me power in prayer as I pray for myself, those I love, and others in my Fellowship and church.

When I commit my life to the Lord for the whole day, His eternal, almighty power will protect me and accomplish every good thing for others and me. When I take time for prayer and a daily Quiet Time, I will experience in full reality the joyful presence and power of the Almighty Jesus, almighty to save!

Prayer for Today

Dear Jesus, in holy love you sacrificed your life to conquer sin in me. Fill me with your love and give me an abiding sense of your presence so I will be changed and be an example of your saving grace. Dear Jesus, I praise you for the work you did in me yesterday, especially for the serenity that came from spending time with you. Today, I pray that you will give me the courage to become willing to remove these additional defects and weaknesses which your Holy Spirit has shown me; so I can be rid of...

The Sixth Step to Serenity

Day 39
I Can Become More Like God

Were entirely ready to have God remove all these defects of character.
—The Sixth Step

I am the Lord your God; consecrate yourselves and be holy, because I am holy.
—Leviticus 11:44

I need to learn how to give God's holiness the place it needs in my faith and life. To practice living in God's Holy Presence, I need to read God's Holy Word as I pray. O God, give me the power to live according to all the truth I am learning.

In the Book of Leviticus, God commands us five times, "Be holy, for I am holy." The Apostle Paul prays for all believers: "May he strengthen your hearts so that you will be blameless and holy in the presence of our God and Father when our Lord Jesus comes with all his holy ones. For God did not call us to be impure, but to live a holy life. The one who calls you is faithful and he will do it" (1 Thessalonians 3:13; 4:7; 5:24). God will make me holy, like Him, and He will give me the true and lasting joy and serenity that comes from being and living like Him.

Only by knowing God as the Holy One will I become holy. I will not obtain this knowledge of God unless I spend some time alone with Him in prayer. I need a daily Quiet Time to appreciate and experience all that God wants to do for me, and for others through me. I need to take time and allow the holiness of God to shine on and within me.

How can anyone obtain intimate knowledge of a person with extraordinary wisdom unless he associates with that person and remains under his influence? Likewise, how can God make me holy, if I will not take time to come under the power of His glory and holiness? Only through prayer and meditation upon the Word of God can I come under the power and influence of God and get to know His holiness. Someone has said, "No one can expect to make progress in holiness if he is not often and long alone with God." Along with many others in the Program, I have found this to be true.

Holiness is the most profound word in the Bible. John heard the four living creatures call out: "Holy, holy, holy is the Lord God Almighty" (Revelation 4:8). By simply thinking, reading, and hearing, I will not understand or partake in the Holiness of God. I need to be alone with God and pray: "Let your holiness, O Lord, shine more and more into my heart that I may become holy like you."

Prayer for Today

Dear Father, make me ready to have all of my character defects removed. As I turn more of my life over to you, fill me with your holiness, and the serenity that can come from living a holy life for you. By your Holy Spirit, transform my life daily, so my character will become more holy as you are holy. Today, I pray that you will help me become more and more willing to remove from my character those defects that are still keeping me from manifesting your holy love to others, please help me face and remove . . .

Day 40
Receiving the Fullness of God

Were entirely ready to have God remove all these defects of character.
—The Sixth Step

Your attitude should be the same as that of Christ Jesus
—Philippians 2:5

Because Jesus humbled himself and obeyed to the death, even death on a cross, His Father exalted Him. Above everything else, the obedient spirit of Jesus needs to become the chief characteristic of my disposition. I need to pray for Jesus' attitude toward life and death, and ask Him to give me His viewpoint on everything.

As I prepare to ask God to remove all of my character defects, am I also willing to obey God in all things? Could my major character defect turn out to be my unwillingness to try to obey God in everything? Am I really willing to pray, "O God, help me always to do your will"? Can I trust that walking in God's will keeps me on the joyful path of lasting peace?

An employee who habitually disobeyed his manager and hurt others would get fired from his job. Likewise, as a child of God, I should not habitually disobey God. Should God treat me any differently from the way an honest employer would treat a dishonest employee out to do harm to himself and others? If I just confessed the same trespasses again and again everyday, and did not take any action to change or ask God to give me the power to do differently, refused to surrender to God and pray for God to remove my character defects, how should I expect God to treat me? Has God always been far more loving and gracious than I deserve? Can I admit this fact and love Him even more for His grace?

The Holy Spirit desires to possess me fully. To receive the fullness of His loving presence, I need to surrender fully to His rule over my life. The Scriptures command me to follow the Spirit's leading and walk by the Spirit. To have a right relationship to the Holy Spirit, I need to pray for His constant guidance and help in all my decision making. Obeying God from a heart full of love is the most important factor in my whole relationship to God.

It is one thing for me to want to be rid of those habits, addictions, compulsions, weaknesses, and dependencies that are destroying me, and quite another thing for me to be ready to obey God in all things. The difference means turning from self-centeredness to God-centeredness. Through living a God-centered life I will find the serenity that following the Program promises.

Prayer for Today

Dear God, if I am not committed to fully obeying you and the Scriptures, I will get confused by the conflicting "leadings" and "feelings" I may get in times of meditation. I will soon begin to follow my feelings instead of your spoken word in the Bible. By following my emotions, I will soon be led away from your Holy Presence and the serenity that following you gives. Help me to take seriously the meaning of this new Step in my journey of recovery. Today, show me what else may be standing in the way of my having a deeper relationship with you, so I will be more willing to remove from my life . . .

Day 41
Prayer Leads Me to Victory

Were entirely ready to have God remove all these defects of character.
—The Sixth Step

What a wretched man I am! Who will rescue me from this body of death? Thanks be to God—through Jesus Christ our Lord.
—Romans 7:24, 25

My way of living has a mighty influence over my prayers. If I am worldly and self-seeking, my prayers will be powerless and unanswered. Is there a conflict between my life and prayer? Am I ready for God to make any changes He finds necessary, so my prayers will be more effective? Am I ready to have every character defect removed? Am I ready to avoid every situation and flee from every opportunity that will tempt me to do wrong?

I cannot allow the ways of the world to have the upper hand in my life. I need God to rule and exercise His mighty influence over me. Prayer can conquer sin. Prayer can overcome temptation. In prayer, I will yield myself completely to God. My entire life can be brought under the control of God through prayer. If I receive the Lord Jesus and the Holy Spirit into my life, then through prayer they will change and renew my life; they will purify and sanctify me. O God, help me to fully consecrate myself to you this day.

If I am not ready for God to remove my character defects, the rest of my prayer life will be defective. I will be working myself up to pray more and more and be disappointed at the results. Only as God strengthens my spiritual life through my daily surrender to Him will my prayer time joyfully increase. To maintain my serenity, the way I live cannot be disconnected from the way I pray and the One to Whom I pray.

Which has more influence over me, a five minute prayer or my worldly desires? If my prayer life and my desires clash and contend with each other, then I may concentrate more on fulfilling my desires than obeying God. If I give God total control and surrender my heart to Him, then God will come to rule my life through faithful prayer. After I ask God to take full possession of my heart and life, my Quiet Time will become as sacred and powerful as God wants it to be.

Prayer for Today

Dear Father, this prayer takes great courage for me to pray. I am now willing for you to do whatever it takes to make me willing to have you remove all of my character defects. Help me see that my future depends on taking this crucial Step and casting myself wholly into your loving hands. Show me anything else I must do regarding my weaknesses. Show me anything that may be keeping me from experiencing the serenity that only you can give me. Today, help me to be willing to do your will, and to be willing to remove from my life forever this besetting sin of . . .

Day 42
The Sixth Step and the Serenity Prayer

Were entirely ready to have God remove all these defects of character.
—The Sixth Step

*God, grant me the serenity to accept the things I cannot change, **the** **courage** to change the things I can, and the wisdom to know the difference.*
—The Serenity Prayer

Have I not commanded you? Be strong and courageous. Do not be terrified; do not be discouraged, for the LORD your God will be with you wherever you go.
—Joshua 1:9

We may be so addicted to some of our cherished bad habits that we do not believe we can live without our drugs of choice, unhealthy relationships, unwholesome pleasures, or defects of character. Perhaps we have deceived ourselves into thinking that we need to continue doing some of the things that we know will harm us simply because these things seem to help us cope "for now." Once we begin to grow spiritually through walking The Twelve Steps Journey, we become more serene, secure, and able to break away from our compulsions, dependencies, and character defects. Even though we have almost completed half of the twelve Prayer Steps to Serenity, we still need to trust more in God and ask God to help us come to that place of total reliance on Him, where we can become completely ready for God to remove all of our defects of character.

When we consider how much we have come to depend on unhealthy habits and relationships to get us through the day, we come to realize how much The Serenity Prayer means to us when we pray for *"the courage* to change the things we can." A good character trait is choosing to live courageously; making the courageous choice a matter of habit and a settled conviction when tempted. Acting courageously can become the way we almost instinctively choose when we are tempted to cave in under the pressure to use again or act compulsively. Acting compulsively, instead of thoughtfully and prayerfully according to God's purposes for us, is one of the character defects we pray that God will help us become ready to remove. It takes courage to face *all* of our character defects, admit them to God and one other person, and then become ready for God to remove them.

Only God can remove our character defects. We have discovered that we cannot remove them ourselves; for if we could have removed our defects, we would have removed them long ago with all the resolutions to do better that we made over and over again. We had "the best" intentions, and we made "the most" sincere efforts, but we could not do what only God can do for us and in us. We have found it difficult to believe that God can meet our needs in the best way, when for so long we have depended on other things or people to relieve our pain or give us temporary pleasures. With a measure of faith, and while praying to God for more faith, we pray The Serenity Prayer especially for *"the courage."*

Joshua had many fears within and foes without. Surrounded by his enemies, God called him to lead His people and defeat them. To do so, Joshua needed to obey God's command to be strong and courageous. Likewise, when we face our enemies within and without, God commands us to be strong and courageous. God will not do for us what He commands us to do for ourselves, but God does promise us (as He promised Joshua) that He will be with us wherever we go. Moreover, when we ask God, He will give us the strength we need to be strong. The Twelve Steps are a program of action. God takes action in our behalf, and God expects us to take action in our behalf, and do so courageously. Through daily prayer, God will give us the faith and hope we need to be courageous. God will remove our character defects and replace them with the good character traits that come from trusting in and obeying God day by day. Joshua overcame his fears, and with God's help we can have the confidence we need to complete this step.

Prayer for Today

Dear God, for a long time I felt I was a victim, doomed to suffer at the hands of others and needing dependencies that I knew were destroying my life and peace. Now I know that I was deceived. What I thought were just bad habits were actually manifestations of my character defects. To overcome, I needed to be strong and courageous. I needed the courage to change the things I could change. I needed to know what I could change and not burden myself with false guilt and feelings of inadequacy over those things I could not change. I am learning that many things in this life I cannot face or do without Your guidance and help. Today, please give me the courage I need to . . .

Prayer Step Principle

True prayer submits to the will of God and says, "your will be done" (Matthew 6:10). Therefore, the people of the Lord in humility are to lay themselves and their prayers, and all that they have, at the foot of their God to be disposed of by Him as He in His heavenly wisdom sees best.

John Bunyan in *How to Pray in the Spirit*

The Twelve Steps Journey
Step 6 Workbook

Were entirely ready to have God remove all these defects of character.
—The Sixth Step

We also rejoice in our sufferings, because we know that suffering produces perseverance; perseverance, character; and character, hope. And hope does not disappoint us, because God has poured out his love into our hearts by the Holy Spirit, whom he has given us.
—Romans 5:3-5

Things I have learned about God and prayer:

Things I have learned about myself:

What I have learned about my will power:

What I have learned about others and my relationship with them:

My prayer requests and answers to prayer:

Prayer for Today

God, grant me the Serenity to accept the things I cannot change, the Courage to change the things I can, and the Wisdom to know the difference. Lord God, help me today to . . .

Day 43
The Seventh Step to Serenity

Humbly asked Him to remove our shortcomings.
—The Seventh Step

Ask and it will be given to you; seek and you will find; knock and the door will be opened to you. For everyone who asks receives; he who seeks finds; and to him who knocks, the door will be opened.
—Matthew 7:7, 8

As God leads me through The Twelve Steps, and as I pray over and do whatever the Prayer Steps to Serenity require, God makes me more humble. God has never, and will never, embarrass me. Whereas my dependencies brought humiliation, God brings jubilation. God will never disgrace me. The destructive idols that I have served will always eventually degrade me. Chemicals or practices that promised me success, pleasure, enlightenment, or happiness have led to shortcomings that brought me so low I had to look up to see bottom. In desperation,

I sought God. I now ask Him to remove my shortcomings and dependencies on anyone or anything other than God and His loving, infinite, merciful, forgiving, and almighty power.

Following The Twelve Steps will help me overcome the dishonor of abuse or abusing, and help me live without self-pity or arrogance. I will no longer live tooting my own horn for fear no one else will. After God removes my shortcomings, people will see me treating them more courteously and respectfully. They will know by the changes in me that I have been spending more and more time with a redeeming and transforming God. God alone will receive all the credit for my recovery as I humbly praise Him publicly and privately for His work in overcoming my defects of character and destructive habits.

The Sixth Step led me to be ready for God to remove my shortcomings. Now in the Seventh Step, I will turn to God and ask God to remove them all. As I pray, I will need to be specific in my requests. My specific prayers will show God that I understand my shortcomings and know these flaws are not just slips but real character defects that God alone can remove. I have confessed, and will confess, that I have been unwilling or unable to overcome certain habits and practices. Now, I want God to take over my entire life and conquer the individual defects that concern me.

As God gives me victory over some of my shortcomings, I know He will prevail over them all. I need to surrender daily to God, asking God for power for that day to do His will in all things. I thank God for the triumph over temptation and sin that He has promised through faith in Jesus.

Prayer for Today

God, grant me the Serenity to accept the things I cannot change, the Courage to change the things I can, and the Wisdom to know the difference. Lord God, help me today to . . .

The Seventh Step to
Serenity

Day 44
God's Wonderful Promises to Me

Humbly asked Him to remove our shortcomings.
—The Seventh Step

For I will forgive their wickedness and will remember their sins no more.
—Hebrews 8:12

The Lord Jesus Christ died to atone for my sins. By His grace through faith, He will destroy the power of sin over my life. He came to give me free access to God's presence. Therefore, in His Name I can secure God's favor when I pray. He came to remove my shortcomings and give me a new heart. He freed me from the power of sin and filled me with the Holy Spirit. The Spirit now breathes in me the power to overcome all my temptations and obey God in all things.

I will put my trust in Jesus for the forgiveness of my sins and claim the fullness of His other promise—that He will remove all my shortcomings.

He will remove them, and He will cleanse me. He will give me such a delight in and love for God and God's law that I will rejoice in God's commandments. God will give me such power in prayer that I will focus more on God, on loving God and loving others, instead of merely on my own problems and self-centered concerns.

I have come a long way from breaking the rules and ignoring the consequences. I now see why all of God's standards are right and reasonable, and that I need Him to remove my defects of character so I can do right. If I ask Him, Jesus will write God's law on my heart by the power of His Spirit so I will know how to act in every situation—totally trusting in Him for everything.

God asked Abraham "Is anything too hard for the Lord?" (Genesis 18:14). If I will set aside my preconceived opinions and believe in the almighty power of God and His desire to help me, He will remove my shortcomings.

Prayer for Today

Dear Father, help me remember that my forgiveness and the removal of my sins (as far as the East is from the West) came at the cost of your Son's life. He suffered and died in my place. Therefore, I am certain that He is willing to live in me and overcome all my shortcomings to grant me serenity. Thank you God for all the promises in your Word that I am just beginning to understand. Today, a major shortcoming oppresses my soul; therefore, for the sake of honoring your Son, I ask you now to remove . . .

The Seventh Step to Serenity

Day 45
God Will Work Wonders in Me

Humbly asked Him to remove our shortcomings.
—The Seventh Step

I pray that out of his glorious riches he may strengthen you with power through his Spirit in your inner being, so that Christ may dwell in your hearts through faith.
—Ephesians 3:16, 17

Only the God who works wonders can help me. If I ask Him in faith, He will remove all my shortcomings. If I lack love, I can go to the Throne of Grace and He will fill me with His love. God is love. Whatever I really need, He will see that I have. If I have unreasonable fears, He will cast out my fears and fill me with the perfect peace of His presence.

The gift of love only comes when Jesus fills my heart with His presence. As I seek God daily in prayer, Jesus will sustain my love for Him. As

Jesus dwells more fully in me, He will lovingly remove all my shortcomings. When I humbly bow before the Throne of Grace and humbly wait and worship there, I will receive the indwelling Spirit and know the love of Christ fully. Knowing Christ and His love will give me confidence in prayer to trust fully in Him to remove my character defects.

I do not seek forgiveness only. I also seek that abundant grace that will help me live continually victorious over sin and temptation. During my time in prayer and meditation on the Word of God, I ask God to fit me for the continual indwelling and guidance of the Holy Spirit. I earnestly pray that I may so live that the love of Christ, which passes all understanding, will be first place in my life. Only by spending time before the Throne of Grace will I ground my life and recovery in the almighty love of God and His transforming presence.

When I have come to really love God and have gotten beyond just talking about my need to love Him, His love will radiate from me to all those around me. The love of Christ in me will reach out and enrich the hearts of those who do not yet know Him, love Him, or follow Him. By grace, through faith and prayer, I will obtain the state of blessedness I seek.

Prayer for Today

Dear Father, strengthen my faith according to the riches of your glory. Show me more of your wonder working power by removing my shortcomings so I can know more of the love of Christ and love others as I ought to love. As I express my love for you and others, may others see your presence and serenity in me. May your Spirit draw them to you by working through me. May they begin to learn the secret of practicing The Twelve Steps Journey that you have given for my recovery. Today, I pray that you will remove my greatest moral weakness; which your Spirit has shown me is . . .

Day 46
God's Love Will Remove My Hatred

Humbly asked Him to remove our shortcomings.
—The Seventh Step

My command is this: Love each other as I have loved you.
—John 15:12

Jesus' command to love is so difficult to keep that I am often tempted to quit trying. Some people have done some very hateful things to others and me. Yet, The Twelve Steps Journey requires that I recognize my own hateful attitudes as shortcomings and character defects that God needs to remove and that I can change with God's help.

As Jesus loves me, His love comes to fill me. As I open more of my heart to Him, He will fill me more and more. As He dwells within me, He casts out my character defects—if I humbly ask Him. Day-by-day through prayer and asking Him to remove these destructive attitudes, compulsions and feelings, I find myself improving and learning to pray even for my enemies. As I spend more time with Jesus, I gradually begin to take on His loving and forgiving character.

If I say I love God and hate my brother, I am a liar. If I hate my fellow-man, this is a sure sign I do not truly love God. I must ask God to remove this character defect.

Jesus really means, "Love one another as I have loved you." Through the Holy Spirit, that He sends to live in every believer, He will enable me to love others. As I love others in the power of Jesus' love, they will also grow strong in love. As they grow strong in love, I will have powerful evidence that Jesus dwells in me and the Father has shed His love abroad in my heart.

I want to bow at the Throne of Jesus. I want to love, worship and adore Him for His wonderful grace. By His love, He seeks to transform me and make me more like himself. As He lives in my heart, He will cast out all hatred, give me a wonderful love for others, and prove to the world that God is definitely in our midst.

Prayer for Today

Dear Jesus, help me to see that my biggest character defect may be my attitude toward others. Help me to see those I still despise as you see them, with your compassionate desire that everyone allow you to transform them into your image. Help me to see that they need the serenity that you are giving me daily through faith in you. Today, I pray that you will give me love for my enemies and remove my hatred for or anger toward . . .

Day 47
My Whole Life Depends on Jesus

Humbly asked Him to remove our shortcomings.
—The Seventh Step

Do not let your hearts be troubled. Trust in God; trust also in me.
—John 14:1

Jesus taught His disciples to pray to and believe in Him with the same perfect confidence they had in God the Father. They could trust their heavenly Father and they could trust Him. They could trust in His perfect love and grace, and they could trust in the Holy Spirit as He lived in them and taught them how to pray.

I need to ask God to remove those flaws in me that influence me to visualize a god compatible with my character defects. If I imagine or even serve a god with moral defects instead of the perfect God, I may comfort my conscience until it no longer speaks to me of my wrongs. But, if I am to really change for the better, I need to ask God to remake me into His moral image—into the perfect image of His Son.

The deity of Jesus is the rock upon which my faith depends. The Lord Jesus, as a man, partook of my nature, but without any defects of character or moral flaws—He lived without sin. He is indeed true God. Just as divine power raised Jesus from the dead, so His divine omnipotence can work in me all that I need to overcome my weaknesses.

I need to humble myself and ask Jesus to remove any character defects in me. I do not want any character defects to keep me from seeing God as He is. Jesus said, "Blessed are the pure in heart for they will see God" (Matthew 5:8). As Jesus removes my flaws and creates a pure heart within me, I will see God as He really is, and I will take time to bow before Jesus and worship Him as I worship the Father.

I need to be conscious of Jesus' presence as my Almighty Redeemer, who is able to save me from my sins, cleanse me, and empower me to do right. As I seek Jesus daily, I will come to love Him as the Mighty God and place all my confidence in Him as my Strength. I need to ask Jesus to give me a direct, definite, unceasing faith in His power at work in me. As I rely more upon Him to remake my soul, He will show me all that He can do to transform my life.

Prayer for Today

Dear Jesus, when so many say that you were just a good teacher, help me to see you as you really are, as Lord and Savior. It is not just from practicing The Twelve Steps Journey that I will maintain serenity, but also from knowing you better day by day. Help me learn more about you through your many names in the Bible that reveal your nature and character. Reveal to me what flesh and blood can never reveal—that you are the Christ, the Son of the living God. Today, dear Jesus, fill me with your loving presence so there is no longer any room in my life for . . .

Day 48
I Know God Will Help Me

Humbly asked Him to remove our shortcomings.
—The Seventh Step

Now faith is being sure of what we hope for and certain of what we do not see.
—Hebrews 11:1

God will not remove all of my character defects all at once. He will usually remove them slowly and only one defect at a time. Their slow removal can encourage my steady spiritual growth and keep me relying daily on God for absolutely everything. Jesus trained His disciples to expect delay sometimes when they prayed. He encouraged them to keep on trusting in God and persevering in prayer until His mighty power brought them the answer they needed.

When the answers to my prayers do not come according to my timing, the promises I firmly trust can appear to be false. In the trial of "unanswered prayer," I need to wait on God with patience. Through patience in times of trial, God will purify and strengthen my faith. By faith, I need to claim for myself and hold onto the promises of God until I receive the fulfillment of all that God promises in the Bible.

To strengthen our faith and help us grow spiritually, God requires persevering prayer. Jesus taught that if an unfriendly, selfish neighbor would give someone what he needed when he kept asking, then God would give far more—because God is an unselfish, loving, Heavenly Father. When God delays in giving me what I need, He is teaching me to live with Him in undoubting faith and trust—to indeed become His friend, and not just want the things He has to give. God may delay in removing my shortcomings, but by His grace and through trusting prayer each day, He will eventually remove them all.

Jesus did not promise to heal my every physical disease in this life, but He did promise to save me from my sins. As I go to Him each day, I need to tell Him specifically the character flaws that I want Him to remove, and then by faith begin thanking Him for their removal. As the Spirit of Jesus works in me, I will see myself growing in obedience and gaining power over the temptations and compulsions that once had absolute power and control over me.

Prayer for Today

Dear Jesus, keep me patient when I wait in prayer. Help me maintain my serenity when I am not experiencing your presence as I would like in my Quiet Time. I have much that needs improving. Work in me and make me into the person you want me to be. As I think about all my shortcomings, if I could have only one of them removed immediately, today, I pray that you would remove . . .

Day 49
The Seventh Step and the Serenity Prayer

Humbly asked Him to remove our shortcomings.
—The Seventh Step

God, grant me the serenity to accept the things I cannot change, the courage **to change** *the things I can, and the wisdom to know the difference.*
—The Serenity Prayer

Jesus said: "I tell you the truth, unless you change and become like little children, you will never enter the kingdom of heaven. Therefore, whoever humbles himself like this child is the greatest in the kingdom of heaven."
— Matthew 18:3, 4

The Twelve Steps Journey leads me into a better understanding of myself and Step by Step makes me more humble. After I humbly ask Him, God gives me the courage to change the things I can change. However, as I make improvements in my way of living, I almost become proud of my achievements—forgetting that my Higher Power was the only One giving me the courage I lacked.

Early in my recovery, I also recognized that no matter how much I prayed for the courage to change some things, I needed more than courage. I humbly needed to admit that even with all the courage in the world, I still could not remove all of my shortcomings—not all by myself. I discovered the importance of that very first word and the very first person mentioned in The Serenity Prayer—God. I learned that my only hope was asking God to remove my shortcomings—trusting that God would continue the good work that He had begun in me, even before I took my First Step in the Program.

When I continue to humble myself before God, I move ahead in the Program. Through prayer, God restores my serenity. Through prayer, God gives me His power when I begin to crumble under the pressures of my old habits and temptations. As I pray and trust in God, He slowly changes the things I cannot change, and I experience the spiritual growth and character development that following The Twelve Steps promises. My love for God increases daily as I thank Him for substantially healing me and removing my addictions, compulsions, and obsessions—one day at a time.

As I continue to practice the Prayer Steps to Serenity in all of my affairs, I need to remind myself that no matter how much I want to change some things, no matter how much I want *the courage* to change some things, my highest endeavor must be humbling myself even more and asking God to remove those shortcomings that only God has the power to change and take away completely. As I remain humble in prayer, God will show me what I can do with His help, what God and I can do together, and what only God can do for me.

Jesus promised that I could change and become like a little child. Whatever He asks me to do He will give me the power to do through prayer—if I need His strength to obey Him, I ask Him for His strength. Little children depend totally on others to meet their needs. I need to become so humble that I learn how to depend on God for everything, without this becoming another unhealthy dependency. Walking in the Prayer Steps helps me find and maintain a healthy dependency on God as my Higher Power. I can depend on God to help me find, maintain, and restore healthy relationships. I can rely totally on God to meet my needs and help me find the right things to do with my life. I can trust God to remove my unhealthy dependencies and obsessions. I am convinced that God will teach me how to pray as I ought to pray for myself and others. I believe God will answer The Serenity Prayer when I begin to pray this prayer in the midst of extreme circumstances. I can depend on God to make me over into the kind of person that God wants me to become. Such total dependence on my Creator, Redeemer, and Friend will eliminate either immediately or in God's timing the unhealthy dependencies that I unknowingly substituted for depending on the true God as a little child of God.

When I think about those in my Fellowship who have gone the furthest in their spiritual development, I recognize that they are also the most humble. Those who are the greatest help to me and others are also the most humble about the help they give. They do not help me and others because they think they are better than the rest of us. No. They have walked the Steps and they know what we need. Their kind and merciful words and actions toward us flow through the loving and humble spirit that God has given them as they walk The Twelve Steps Journey. I pray that God will someday help me to humbly help others as I have been helped.

Prayer for Today

Dear God, you are my Creator and loving heavenly Father. Your Son is my Savior, Lord, Elder Brother, and Friend. Your Spirit lives in my heart, gives me power, and teaches me how to love you, others, and even myself. O God, Father, Son, and Holy Spirit, you are everything to me and I depend on you for everything. Help me to always come to you humbly as a little child. Help me to pray to you when I feel the pressures to begin doing again those things that I have renounced with your help. Remove from me all of my shortcomings; and as I think of one of my worst shortcomings right now, I humbly ask you to remove as soon as possible my shortcoming of . . .

Prayer Step Principle

If you mean to pray effectively, you must pray a great deal. . . . You cannot prevail in prayer without renouncing all your sins. You must not only recall them to mind, and repent of them, but you must actually renounce them, and purpose in your heart to give them up forever.

Charles G. Finney in *Principles of Prayer*

The Twelve Steps Journey
Step 7 Workbook

Humbly asked Him to remove our shortcomings.
—The Seventh Step

Therefore, get rid of all moral filth and the evil that is so prevalent and humbly accept the word planted in you, which can save you.
—James 1:21

Things I have learned about God and prayer:

Things I have learned about myself:

What I have learned about how my shortcomings can be eliminated:

What I have learned about others and my relationship with them:

My prayer requests and answers to prayer:

Prayer for Today

God, grant me the Serenity to accept the things I cannot change, the Courage to change the things I can, and the Wisdom to know the difference. Lord God, help me today to . . .

Day 50
The Eighth Step to Serenity

Made a list of all persons we had harmed and became willing to make amends to them all.

—The Eighth Step

Zacchaeus stood up and said to the Lord, "Look, Lord! Here and now I give half of my possessions to the poor, and if I have cheated anybody out of anything, I will pay back four times the amount." Jesus said to him, "Today salvation has come to this house."

—Luke 19:8, 9

The first seven Steps helped me get right with God. Daily prayer steps help me stay right. Through daily prayer, God shows me new and wonderful possibilities for living. Through daily reading of the Scriptures, God shows me His desires for all of my personal relationships.

I thank God for not requiring me to make everything right with others before coming to make things right with Him. God knows that without getting things right with Him first, and without getting His guidance and help, I can never really begin to make things right with others. I need to be willing to make amends to those I have harmed, but first things first.

Once I am right with God, I will have God's help in restoring a right relationship with others where possible or advisable. By working the Eighth Step, I will explore how to heal some relationships, how to make restitution, how to decide if my efforts to make amends will be accepted, and how I will accept rejection of my efforts (if rejected).

As I think of all the new beginnings I have made with others, almost incidentally as I have worked through the first seven Steps of this journey, I am encouraged to press ahead with the Eighth. Though I still face some painful regrets, some in my Fellowship have told me about their joyful memories of completing the Steps, and their encouragement has helped me press on to work the Program completely.

Through prayer, God will help me remember and list all the persons I have harmed, and I can pray for each one as I remember each one. I will expand my moral inventory as I focus my attention on the needs and hurts of others instead of on my own needs and pains. Working the Eighth Step will broaden my circle of concern beyond God and myself.

Through prayer, God will help me to be willing to heal relationships. Every time I *become willing* to make amends, I have an answer to my prayers for that person and my attitude toward them. And, I will pray differently for these people as I seek to learn whether or not or how I can make amends to them.

Becoming willing to make amends makes me deal with my deepest feelings of shame and disappointment. After I have become willing to make amends, I am set free. Almost miraculously, I have overcome the fearful anticipation of seeing and speaking to those I have hurt.

Prayer for Today

God, grant me the Serenity to accept the things I cannot change, the Courage to change the things I can, and the Wisdom to know the difference. Lord God, help me today to . . .

Day 51
Some Benefits of Making Amends

Made a list of all persons we had harmed and became willing to make amends to them all.

—The Eighth Step

A new command I give you: Love one another. As I have loved you, so you must love one another.

—John 13:34

Jesus did not need to make amends to anyone for anything He ever did, for He never did anything to harm God or any person. In some mysterious way, when He died on the cross, He made amends for me in ways that I could never do. I could spend the rest of my life trying to make everything right with God and others, and repair all the damage that I have ever done, but I would never be able to get completely right with God and others—or live in the present for the future. I would never be able to move beyond Step Eight or Step Nine and complete the

Program. Thankfully, God does not require me to do the impossible and neither does The Twelve Steps Journey.

Being willing to make amends to everyone is a part of my recovery for spiritual and psychological reasons that only those who have taken the Eighth Step can begin to understand. I found freedom from guilt and resentment, from blaming others for my mistakes, and I began to take responsibility for my life in a more mature way. I found that things no longer hung over my head and accused me of things left undone as they once did.

As I become more like Jesus, and begin to love others as He loves me, I become more willing to make amends wherever I can. I begin to pray for and seek ways to restore broken friendships and relationships. Where I have not yet found a way to make amends with some, I begin to pray for God to bless them and I try to pray specifically. I pray for God to do for them what I cannot do personally. My prayers become more concerned for the welfare of others. I ask God about how I can make up with them or bless them, and not just further my own recovery. I ask God to help me avoid obsessing over this Step or anyone that I feel I need to make amends to or pray for God to bless.

Jesus' command assures me of His power to carry it out. If I ask Him, God will always give me the power to do His will. Otherwise, God will often let me fail when I try to obey Him in my own strength. My failures will teach me to depend on Him moment-by-moment throughout the day. As I think about working this Step, I know I cannot complete it without His love and grace filling my heart.

Prayer for Today

Dear Jesus, dwell in my heart with your divine love. Teach me to love others at all times and in all circumstances. You are the Vine and I am the branch. By remaining in you I find serenity and can bear much good fruit. Give me the love I need for those I have offended, and make me willing to make amends. Today, my broken heart is willing to make amends to this one special person who is on my mind, help me to find a way, if it is your will, to reach out and make amends someday to . . .

The Eighth Step to Serenity

Day 52
Forgiving Helps Me Make Amends

Made a list of all persons we had harmed and became willing to make amends to them all.
—The Eighth Step

And when you stand praying, if you hold anything against anyone, forgive him, so that your Father in heaven may forgive you your sins.
—Mark 11:25

I am tempted to rationalize; then resent people for what they did to me, rather than accept any responsibility for my own actions in relation to them. Maybe for that reason these people are the very last I will think about with regard to making amends. Indeed, I may feel they need to make amends to me and hold a grudge against them until they do. But rationalizing and resenting is only hurting me and slowing down my recovery.

Realizing how I feel about some who have offended me motivates me to think about how I can make amends to everyone I have offended. If I hold grudges against some who have hurt me, I need to ask God to help me to change. If I find it difficult to forgive someone, without their first seeking to make amends to me, I can help someone else by going to them and seeking their forgiveness. I must begin. Eventually, I will forgive everyone who has hurt me.

Refusing to forgive others, whether they try to make amends or not, and refusing to even think about seeking the forgiveness of others by trying to undo the harm I have done them, will interfere with my prayers and recovery. As I become more and more willing to do God's will in this matter, He will give me greater freedom in prayer.

Jesus' love in me motivates me to seek the happiness of others—especially those I have harmed in any way. My hurtful words or actions may be keeping some from coming to God, if they blame God for what I did. Making amends to them may be the answer to their prayers and restore their confidence in God. If I make amends with the love of Jesus in my heart, some may see the love of God for them and come to believe in God and trust in Jesus

Jesus saved me from my addictions and dependencies not just to make me happy. That was only the beginning. Jesus wants me to share His love in words and in the heavenly power of His love in my life.

Prayer for Today

Dear Jesus, as I pray, forgiving others, pour your love into my life so I will be able to bless those I have offended in any way by making amends to them. By making amends to them, may they come to experience the serenity I feel through obeying you in this Step. Search my heart with your Spirit. Today, reveal to me what others may see in me, and then help me to be willing to make amends to these additional people I would rather not speak to . . .

Day 53
I Will Take Up My Cross

Made a list of all persons we had harmed and became willing to make amends to them all.

—The Eighth Step

And anyone who does not take his cross and follow me is not worthy of me. Whoever finds his life will lose it, and whoever loses his life for my sake will find it.

—Matthew 10:38, 39

The Eighth Step leads me to even greater humility than when I took my moral inventory in Step Four. Now I need to be willing to face the person I have wronged, confess my shortcomings to them, and offer to make things right if I can. This will be especially difficult if I believe they have also wronged me and are undeserving of my going to them to make amends. I need to pray for God to give me the willingness to complete this Step.

As a believer in Jesus, with almost every Step I take He requires me to take up my cross and follow Him. Every Step requires more of my self-life to die so God can live in and rule my life. When I pick up my cross to make amends, I die to self-pleasing and self-exaltation, and God gives me additional inner peace, power and happiness. Each time I die to self and selfishness, I find it easier to pray, because I am becoming more like my heavenly Friend and Companion.

The cross is an instrument of execution: I need the death of my self-centeredness. Until I die to living supremely for myself, I will not humble myself enough to make amends to those I may have harmed who do not suspect my shortcomings. I may not need to make amends to them directly, or I may need to be anonymous as I make amends, or I may just need to pray for God to do for them what I cannot do. But, right now, I only need to pray for God to help me become willing to make amends. I know that after I have taken this Step, God will also give me the wisdom and the power to take the next one—in His perfect timing.

Prayer for Today

Dear Father, many of the truths I have been learning from The Twelve Steps, the teachings of Jesus, and those in my Fellowship are like little seeds. Make them germinate in my heart and reveal their full meaning to my mind. May your truths be Seeds of Serenity in my life. Make me ready to hear, understand and obey your truth fully. I am struggling with how I can make amends, but I see that is moving too far ahead of this Step. My real struggle is to be willing to make amends to everyone. My lack of a willing heart is my real problem. Today, O Lord, take away any unwillingness to make amends as I think of . . .

The Eighth Step to Serenity

Day 54
Willing to Give Up Everything

Made a list of all persons we had harmed and became willing to make amends to them all.

—The Eighth Step

In the same way, any of you who does not give up everything he has cannot be my disciple.

—Luke 14:33

Jesus does not require me to take a vow of poverty and live off others or welfare to be His disciple. Indeed, many who have come to know Jesus, or who have walked The Twelve Steps Journey, have overcome poverty and the need to depend on others instead of God.

Jesus does not want me to consider my possessions as my own, but as gifts from God to use to bless others as well as myself. I am not to be self-centered or selfish when I see the needs of others, but ask God how or if I can help them.

The Journey requires that I become willing to make amends to those I have wronged. This may require giving back something I have stolen, or returning money I have acquired by dishonest or unethical means. After I have given back all that I possess to God, it will be easier for me to accept the idea of making restitution wherever God shows me the need to do this.

Jesus Christ claims all from me. Then He undertakes to satisfy my every need and to give a hundred times more than I give up. This may not always mean material blessings, but it does mean spiritual satisfaction and serenity. As I think about what I had to give up with each Step, and thank God for the many blessings each renunciation of my selfishness brought, I know that through Jesus Christ my spiritual life will get better and better (and quite often the material blessings will also be given with abundance beyond expectation).

As I learn what it means to believe Christ is my life, I will count all things as loss for the excellence of knowing Jesus Christ as my Lord. In the path of following and loving Him, I am willing to sacrifice all to make room in my life for the One who is more than everything that God created.

Prayer for Today

Dear Jesus, come into my life and enrich my immortal spirit. Help me to consider everything I have surrendered for you as my highest privilege instead of a burdensome obligation. Give me the strength to give up anything that stands in the way of my serenity. Today, help me to see what I must give up to make amends, and help me to be willing to give up what is necessary to make amends to . . .

The Eighth Step to Serenity

Day 55
Willing to Face What I Lack

Made a list of all persons we had harmed and became willing to make amends to them all.

—The Eighth Step

Jesus looked at him and loved him. "One thing you lack," he said. "Go, sell everything you have and give to the poor, and you will have treasure in heaven. Then come, follow me."

—Mark 10:21

If my recovery seems to be slowing, and if my serenity seems to be slipping away, perhaps I am having difficulty facing all that the Eighth Step requires. In the depth of my heart, I need to become willing to make amends, and I need to look honestly at what that may require. Am I willing to sacrifice my prestige, power, or position to make things right with those I have offended, especially if this may come at great personal cost? I may not have "hit bottom" before beginning my recovery, so completing the Eighth and Ninth Steps may be particularly difficult for me. Yet, if I do not keep walking The Twelve Steps Journey—one day at a time—I know I could fall back into my destructive compulsions and dependencies.

By myself, I cannot complete the Eighth Step. Thank God, the Holy Spirit will give me the strength I need to go on. Jesus promised, "all things are possible with God" (Mark 10:27). The Eighth Step reveals how much I need God for my recovery. Christ's Spirit in me will make me willing to sacrifice my self or my possessions to restore in some way what I have destroyed.

When Peter confessed Jesus as Lord, Jesus declared that he could only do that by divine teaching and the power of God. Only by divine power will I be able to accept what the Eighth Step requires. I need to pray daily for God to give me the willingness to do whatever He wants, and the wisdom to see what He requires. No one has ever naturally completed the Eighth Step without the help of God.

Some have sought to walk the walk or follow Christ without seeking God's power through prayer, and they have failed. Some have felt that serenity was beyond their reach and have given up, without realizing that they needed Jesus Christ as their Higher Power to enable to do all that The Twelve Steps Journey requires.

Prayer for Today

Dear God, help me to put my trust in you as the living God who is willing to work in my heart, to help me become willing to do your will. Show me what your precise will is; especially when I think of my need to be willing to share with those I have failed to help in the past. Work such a change in me that they may see the serenity of your presence in my life as I make amends; that they might want this serenity also, if they too are suffering from character defects and weaknesses. Today, help me to be willing to make amends for failing to help . . .

Day 56
The Eighth Step and the Serenity Prayer

Made a list of all persons we had harmed and became willing to make amends to them all

—The Eighth Step

*God, grant me the serenity to accept the things I cannot change, the courage to change **the things** I can, and the wisdom to know the difference.*

—The Serenity Prayer

All of you, live in harmony with one another; be sympathetic, love as brothers, be compassionate and humble. Do not repay evil with evil or insult with insult, but with blessing, because to this you were called so that you may inherit a blessing. For, "Whoever would love life and see good days must keep his tongue from evil and his lips from deceitful speech. He must turn from evil and do good; he must seek peace and pursue it. For the eyes of the Lord are on the righteous and his ears are attentive to their prayer."

— 1 Peter 3:8-12

I can pray for the Holy Spirit to help me make a complete list of all the people I have harmed in any way. As I do so, I can also pray for the Holy Spirit to show me the things I did wrong and what I can or cannot do to make things right with each person. The Holy Spirit can give me the courage to change the things I can, and since I cannot change the past, that means the Holy Spirit can show me the right things to do in the future that might in some way reverse the effects of the harm I did. Making this list as complete as possible will help me become willing to make amends according to the Spirit's leading. In my list, I will need to be specific about some of the things I did that caused harm to the persons I seek to bless when I make amends to them.

As I begin to list all the persons I have harmed, I need to be careful and avoid trying to justify the things I did that harmed them. Left unchecked by the Holy Spirit, I could begin to magnify and resent some of the things they did to me. I could become indignant by imagining how they may have done harmful things to me first. I could begin to feel that I was justified in striking back at them and then delete them from my list. And yet, if I take this shortcut, I will not enjoy the serenity that the prayer steps offer. By taking shortcuts, my spiritual progress will slowly come to a halt and I may return to my compulsive actions and dependencies.

Working the Program includes my refusing to repay evil with evil and insult with insult. Even if I think I punished someone else justifiably, I might have actually been repaying evil with evil and doing them harm. I need to include these people on my list and become willing to make amends to them. However, I will also need to pray and ask the Holy Spirit to show me how and if I am to make an effort toward making amends to these people. The Spirit may show me that my willingness to make amends is enough toward some—at least at this time. Perhaps the Spirit can use some of the hurtful things I did with a wrong intention to help them make the changes in their lives that they need to make. I can pray this will be so.

As I make my list, I can do so without crushing and overwhelming regrets if I begin to think of ways I can bless or bring happiness to the persons I harmed. God called me into the Program so He could bless me and I could bless others. As I bless others, I open my life more and more to the work of God and to receiving His blessings. True joy can fill my heart as I think of the things I can do that will bring a greater happiness to those

I harmed—a blessing greater than the harm my actions caused. I can only bring this glorious blessing to the people I have harmed if I pray for the Holy Spirit to show me exactly what I can do and when I should do it.

Those in my Fellowship who seem the happiest and most serene are those who express love and sympathy toward others. I need love and sympathy toward those I have harmed. If they have also harmed me, I will need to pray for the Holy Spirit to give me the love and sympathy that God has for them. If I want to truly help others as I help myself when making amends, I will need to develop the virtues of compassion for others and humility. If I express even a hint of arrogance or personal pride over my success in the Program when I make amends, then those I am seeking to bless may refuse my overtures and my relationship with them may become worse instead of better. If I approach those on my list with the goal of restoring harmony, even though I may not desire or seek to reestablish a relationship with them, then I will more easily achieve the goals I seek—that of blessing them and inheriting the blessings that flow from completing the Eighth and Ninth Steps.

Prayer for Today

Dear God, I pray today that your Holy Spirit will guide and direct my thoughts as I make a list of all those I have harmed. Fill me with love for each one. Grant me the spirit of forgiveness for each one who has harmed me. Help me to assess accurately and exactly the extent of the harm I have caused. Help me to be willing to make amends to each person that goes beyond what strict justice might require. Help me to be merciful as you are merciful. May I learn to focus my thoughts and prayers on blessing each one even more than I think they deserve. And now, I pray about the most difficult amend for me to make as I pray specifically for . . .

Prayer Step Principle

Right prayer must come from what the soul apprehends in the light of the Holy Spirit. . . . The prayers that ascend to heaven are the prayers that are sent there by the Holy Spirit: only this prayer is effective.

John Bunyan in *How to Pray in the Spirit*

The Twelve Steps Journey
Step 8 Workbook

Made a list of all persons we had harmed and became willing to make amends to them all.

—The Eighth Step

Fools mock at making amends for sin, but goodwill is found among the upright.

—Proverbs 14:9

Things I have learned about God and prayer:

Things I have learned about myself:

What I have learned about my willingness to will the will of God:

What I have learned about others and my relationship with them:

My prayer requests and answers to prayer:

Prayer for Today

 God, grant me the Serenity to accept the things I cannot change, the Courage to change the things I can, and the Wisdom to know the difference. Lord God, help me today to . . .

Day 57
The Ninth Step to Serenity

Made direct amends to such people wherever possible, except when to do so would injure them or others.

—The Ninth Step

If he has done you any wrong or owes you anything, charge it to me. I, Paul, am writing with my own hand, I will pay it back—not to mention that you owe me your very self.

—Philemon 1:18, 19

I will not make amends to every person on my list, because as I work the Ninth Step I will recognize when making actual amends could be harmful and should be avoided by me. Certainly, I would not want to say or do anything that would hurt another while trying to heal my relationship with someone else. And, I would not want to reestablish a destructive or unhealthy relationship. I need to pray for God's constant guidance as I complete this Step. He must show me the people to reach out to and those to avoid.

Since my life will not end at death, I can pray that when I reach heaven, God will heal my relationship with those who know Him too—the ones I could not reach here. However, by waiting until I get to heaven, I do not want to avoid what God knows I need to do here in this life. I can pray for those I cannot see, and I can pray that everyone I have hurt will come to faith in God and find healing, joy, strength, and eternal life through faith in Jesus Christ.

As I make my "amends list," I need to include the ones who have hurt me. I need to forgive them from my heart (as an act of my will) before I seek to make amends to them. Otherwise, anger or hidden and deeply buried resentments may interfere with the healing we both need. Eventually, good feelings will follow my good decisions and actions.

Making amends may involve learning to love my enemies. God does not require me to have a warm glow of affection or fuzzy feeling for my enemies. But God does want me to pray for them and truly want the very best for them. I can pray that they will fulfill the necessary conditions for them to receive God's blessings. I may need to pray for them to pray through these Prayer Steps too.

I remember how difficult I thought taking the Fifth Step would be—talking to another person about my shortcomings. But the release and joy I experienced afterward made it all worthwhile. I know the same will be true for this Step too.

Completing the Ninth Step restores a balanced mind within and enables a more balanced relationship with others. I will have peace with God, peace with others (in so far at that lies within my ability), and peace of mind. With true peace, I will not return to destructive behaviors or addictions to escape my problems or achieve a false tranquility. By completing the Ninth Step, I will be less likely to say or do things that will require me to make amends again later.

Prayer for Today

God, grant me the Serenity to accept the things I cannot change, the Courage to change the things I can, and the Wisdom to know the difference. Lord God, help me today to . . .

The Ninth Step to Serenity

Day 58
I Will Avoid Making Excuses

Made direct amends to such people wherever possible, except when to do so would injure them or others.
—The Ninth Step

Do everything without complaining or arguing, so that you may become blameless and pure, children of God without fault in a crooked and depraved generation, in which you shine like stars in the universe.
—Philippians 2:14, 15

As my learning increases from studying the Prayer Steps, I may be tempted to put my limited judgment over God's infinite wisdom once again. I may begin to think that I do not need to take the Ninth Step. I can imagine all sorts of scenarios that will give me reasons to skip this Step and move on. I might think my recovery has gone so well that I can drop out now and everything will still be okay. If I rely on myself to move on in the Steps, instead of on my Lord and Savior, I will not complete The Twelve Steps Journey and will hinder my recovery.

I need to be careful and not rationalize that I would only hurt others by taking this Step. This may simply be my way of avoiding something I anticipate will make me uncomfortable or increase my pain. Have I really completed Step Eight? Have I really become willing to make amends to everyone?

The question may be one of pride in human wisdom and achievement. I need to remind myself again and again that humility is the key to my recovery. With humility, I need to go to God in prayer and confess my absolute dependence on Him for taking this Step. I need the Holy Spirit to teach me why the Ninth Step is so important, to give me the power to complete it, and to show me exactly the person or people I must make amends to help.

In working this Step, I will learn to rely even more on God day by day and moment by moment. I will pray without ceasing for the right attitude, actions and words as I make amends. I will pray that my making of amends will bless the person I speak with, and that the Holy Spirit will have prepared their hearts to hear my confession and willingness to repair what I have broken. Lord Jesus, I will depend on you to lead the way.

Prayer for Today

O God, open the way for me to make amends to those who will benefit from my efforts. I do not want to harm anyone with my efforts to achieve serenity. May my amends give us both the serenity that only comes from you and doing your will day by day. Keep me from hypocrisy as I complete this Step. As I make amends, may others receive me in a way that will bring healing, joy and peace to everyone. Today, impress on my mind the name of the first person that I must begin to reach out to; and as I quietly wait on you, show me the outline of your plan for this meeting as I begin to pray for ...

Day 59
The Holy Spirit Will Help Me

Made direct amends to such people wherever possible, except when to do so would injure them or others.

—The Ninth Step

He will bring glory to me by taking from what is mine and making it known to you.

—John 16:14

I can receive the gift of the Holy Spirit through faith in Jesus Christ. When I follow Jesus Christ, the Spirit flows like a river within me. The Spirit flows from the Lord Jesus. The Spirit reveals and imparts Him to me. Jesus sent the Holy Spirit from heaven so He could be glorified in the heart of every believer, and be revealed through the life of His followers. I pray that the Holy Spirit will reveal Christ in me.

The fullness of God dwelt in Jesus Christ in order for Christ, as the life of God, to dwell in His followers. All the life and love, which the Spirit imparts, is in Christ Jesus. My whole spiritual life consists in union with Him. Each new day, I need to praise God that Jesus lives in me, and ask Him to make His presence an abiding reality in my life. I need to rely upon the unseen working of the Holy Spirit in my heart.

With Jesus Christ living in me, I can impart something of His divine life and love to others as I make amends. Some will see the love of Christ shinning forth in me. I will glorify God as people see that my making amends comes from the spiritual renewal Jesus Christ makes in my life.

Some people will understand that my attempts to make things right with them indicate the progress I am making in this journey toward serenity. These people will receive me with an open and forgiving heart. If they can also see that my making amends comes from the work of God in me, they will glorify God, and the Holy Spirit will continue keeping me humble when I do right.

In the life and words of His disciples, antagonistic leaders recognized that His followers had been with Jesus Christ. As I spend daily time with Christ in prayer and meditation upon the Scriptures, the Holy Spirit will work in me so those I fear most may be able see the God of love living and working in me.

Prayer for Today

Oh God, help me overcome all my fears of making amends with those I can, and give me success and serenity as I reach out in love to do so. Today, tell me what I must do so Christ's light can shine forth through me, and prepare the people I list to receive my efforts at making amends to . . .

Day 60
When Christ is My Life

Made direct amends to such people wherever possible, except when to do so would injure them or others.

—The Ninth Step

When Christ, who is your life, appears, then you also will appear with him in glory.

—Colossians 3:4

Many people believe that Jesus died on the cross for them and now lives in heaven. But few believe and live as though Jesus Christ lives within them. The powerlessness of many is mainly due to this narrow view. Do I really believe that the Almighty Lord dwells within me? Do I really believe that His Presence in me is the only source of true serenity?

Believing that Jesus lives in me, and that Christ is my hope for glory, will free me to make amends without fearing the consequences. Through daily prayer, Christ will give me the direction and power to make amends in the best way possible. I will not simply say, "Jesus died for me, so my sins are forgiven," and then ignore making things right with those I have harmed. No. I will say, "Jesus died for me and now lives in me to overcome sin; therefore, by His power I will remedy the harm I have caused."

I need to know, experience, and testify to the truth that Christ lives in me. I cannot use my new found and deepening faith as an excuse for not righting wrongs wherever I can. Jesus lives in me so I can pray to know the right and have the power to do it.

As others receive my offer to restore what I destroyed, they may see that these efforts flow from my desire to live wholly for God in Christ Jesus. Perhaps I can tell them that my efforts to make things right with them come from my desire to have an abiding fellowship with Christ Jesus and do His will in all things.

Some may ask why I am trying to do what they themselves know they need to do. This will give me an opportunity to say that Christ lives in me, and I now want to live for Him. Taking the Ninth Step may give me the opportunity to jump ahead somewhat to working the Twelfth.

Prayer for Today

Dear Jesus, some think Christianity is only an excuse to avoid accountability. Help me show that with you I am now more responsible than ever. Help me show that you want me to make things right wherever I can. Through my efforts, reveal to others that the true way of serenity is following you no matter how difficult the path might seem. Today, help me resolve to be more accountable to . . .

Day 61
Prayer Helps in Making Amends

Made direct amends to such people wherever possible, except when to do so would injure them or others.

—The Ninth Step

And pray in the Spirit on all occasions with all kinds of prayers and requests. With this in mind, be alert and always keep on praying for all the saints.

—Ephesians 6:18

I will not be alone and powerless to make amends when others in my Fellowship pray for me as I take the Ninth Step. I can ask those close to me, who believe in the power of prayer, to prepare the persons I must speak to and prepare me to say and do the right things with the right timing—all in God's power and timing. In The Twelve Steps Journey, we do not need to make amends all alone; we can give prayer support to one another. When we pause quietly in prayer, the Holy Spirit can influence us to pray rightly for one another—and even for people we do not know.

Thank God for this wonder of grace: we can pray down heavenly gifts upon one another. Making the effort to make amends may be the most difficult and responsible action I have ever taken. With God going with me and preparing the way, with God granting me success within as I make the attempt without, I know that He will give me the power to do whatever else the prayer steps require. I do pray today that the serenity I have come to know from practicing these Steps will be with me as I make amends to those I have hurt.

If I fail to pray for others as they make amends, they may suffer from my neglect. If I say I will pray for them, perhaps I need to pray right then, and pray with them for the success of their efforts. In working the Steps, I am not alone.

The Twelve Steps Journey only requires that I make amends *where possible,* and where it will not hurt others. God will show me how to avoid hurting others; either by not making amends to them, or by not making amends to them in the wrong way or at the wrong time. The Ninth Step shows me how much I need to depend on God for everything.

If I cannot make amends personally, I can pray for God to make amends for me. God can restore to others what I cannot restore. God can bless those I have hurt, and give them happiness where I cannot. But I cannot allow prayer to be the substitute for whatever God wants me to do with personal responsibility and action.

Prayer for Today

O God, help me to be a real partner with others who are working the Ninth Step, and help me find some who will pray with me and advise me as I take this Step. Help us to learn and share the secrets to serenity that have helped us. Thank you for not leaving me alone to take this journey all by myself. Today, I want to praise you and thank you for those who pray for me, and now I want to pray for . . .

Day 62
I Will Not Give Up

Made direct amends to such people wherever possible, except when to do so would injure them or others.
—The Ninth Step

Jesus told his disciples ... that they should always pray and not give up.
—Luke 18:1

One of the greatest drawbacks in praying for God's guidance in making amends is the long delay I will sometimes experience in receiving His leading for specific people. This should not surprise me when I remember that God is preparing me to make amends and others to receive my efforts. I must not rush ahead of God to complete these Steps, and God may want me to keep coming back to work this Step as I grow spiritually and am made ready over time. I will not fail to move to the next Step just because God is not ready for me to reach out to everyone on my list at this time and make amends to them.

God may have good reasons for delaying His answers to my prayers. My desire to make amends will grow deeper and stronger as I pray daily for the ones I need to reach out to and bless with my amends. My love for them will grow as God's Spirit leads me in prayer for them. In God's timing, others will see God's love for them in me.

God has put me into a school of prayer: every delay teaches me to keep praying and not give up. As I persevere in prayer, God strengthens my faith. I need to believe that God has a great blessing for me and others from delayed answers.

Above all, God wants to draw me into a closer fellowship with himself. When God delays His answers, I learn that nearness to God and love of God are more important than receiving the answers to my petitions—so I continue in prayer.

I need to remember the blessing Jacob received when God delayed in answering him. He eventually saw God face to face, and as a prince he had power with God and prevailed (see Genesis 32:28-30).

I must not become impatient or discouraged when the answer does not come, but continue in prayer. I can ask myself if my prayer is according to the will and Word of God. I can ask myself if my prayer is in the right spirit and in the name of Jesus Christ. I can ask myself if I have really forgiven others, and especially the person I need to make amends to in taking this Step. If I persevere in prayer, God will teach me what I need to do to secure His answer.

Prayer for Today

Dear Jesus, help me to plead your promises and persevere in prayer so I can have great power with God to achieve blessings for others as well as myself. I know that you have promised serenity to all those who trust in you, so I pray that you will increase my faith in you. Today, as I wait quietly for your leading, show me the names of those I can make amends to before proceeding to take the next Step . . .

Day 63
The Ninth Step and the Serenity Prayer

Made direct amends to such people wherever possible, except when to do so would injure them or others.
—The Ninth Step

*God, grant me the serenity to accept the things I cannot change, the courage to change the things **I can**, and the wisdom to know the difference.*
—The Serenity Prayer

Do not repay anyone evil for evil. Be careful to do what is right in the eyes of everybody. If it is possible, as far as it depends on you, live at peace with everyone.
—Romans 12:17, 18

After I read the Ninth Step, I thought, "I can't." Nevertheless, The Serenity Prayer affirms that "I can." When I read through all the Steps for the first time, for almost every Step I paused and thought, "I can't." However, as I prayed for God to give me the courage and strength I needed, I discovered the truth: "I can!" If I can complete Steps One through Eight, surely I can complete Step Nine—with God's help one Step at a time. If others in my Fellowship have and can complete the Ninth Step; then I can too. The Serenity Prayer gives me the assurance that with sufficient prayer I can complete every Step the Program requires for my full recovery.

With each Step I become more humble. When I worked Step Five, I found it difficult to confess my wrongs to another human being. It will be more difficult to admit exactly what I did wrong to the people I harmed, even with the intention to make things right. However, as I think of each person on my list, most of them know that I hurt them. It will probably not surprise them when I tell them that I wronged them. What may surprise them is my admitting this fact to both them and me. It will probably surprise them even more to learn that I now want to do what I can to make up for the harm I caused them. They will be amazed to learn that I truly want to do what I can to remove the pain I caused them and bring them true joy as I try to restore the happiness I stole from them.

It may be impossible to make amends to some people, for the harm I caused was so long ago that I can no longer find them. If I know where they are, then Step Nine requires that I make amends to them unless "to do so would injure them or others." I need to prayerfully ask God to make it clear to me if my making amends to some of the people on my list would injure them or others. Through prayer, the Holy Spirit will show me the easiest and most important people I need to make amends to first, and the order in which I need to make amends. He may only show me one person at a time, and after I have made amends to that person, He will show me the next person to approach. If I have doubts about whether or not I should make amends to someone, because I do not know if doing so will injure them or others, then I will not make amends until I know that the time and place is right to do so. When the Spirit leads me to make amends, He can do so while removing all doubts about whether I should or not. However, He does not guarantee that the other person will receive my good faith efforts to remedy the harm I caused them.

As I make amends, I need to pray about exactly what God wants me to do. Making amends may not be the same for every person, and will probably be different for each person. While I pray, the Holy Spirit can show me what the other person needs for me to truly repay them for the things I did that hurt them. As I take the Ninth Step for my recovery, I cannot forget that part of my purpose is to bring a blessing to, and not to injure, the person who needs my amends. They need to see that I want to do the right thing insofar at that lies within my ability. Making amends may be something I must do over time as God gives me the resources and strength. As I pray, I can pray for the Holy Spirit to reveal to us both the right things that God wants me to do, so I can do what is right for us both.

When I make amends, my sense of peace and well-being will deepen and God's peace within me will help me live more peaceably with others. I know that others can receive the peace of God through me as I make my amends, and I pray that they will rejoice in this new work of God that they experience through my efforts to restore their loses.

Prayer for Today

O God, I truly want to work the Program fully and completely. Help me know exactly what I am to do as I work the Ninth Step, for I do not want to bring harm to anyone as I seek to repair some of the damage that I have done to others. If I am not to reach out to any person, show me the person that I am not to approach. If the time is not right for me to reach out to them, show me the right time by your Spirit. Prepare their hearts and minds to receive my amends according to your perfect timing. As I pray today, give me the name of the first person you want me to reach out to so I can pray for . . .

Prayer Step Principle

When the signs of the times or the providence of God indicate that a particular blessing is about to be bestowed, we are bound to believe it. . . . When the Spirit of God is upon you and inspires strong desires for a particular blessing, you are bound to pray for it in faith. . . Unless motivated by the Spirit of God, people are not apt to want the right kinds of things.

Charles Finney in *Principles of Prayer*

The Twelve Steps Journey
Step 9 Workbook

Made direct amends to such people wherever possible, except when to do so would injure them or others.
—The Ninth Step

Love does not delight in evil but rejoices with the truth. It always protects, always trusts, always hopes, always perseveres. Love never fails.
—1 Corinthians 13:5-8

Things I have learned about God and prayer:

Things I have learned about myself:

What I have learned about following God in making amends:

What I have learned about others and my relationship with them:

My prayer requests and answers to prayer:

Prayer for Today

God, grant me the Serenity to accept the things I cannot change, the Courage to change the things I can, and the Wisdom to know the difference. Lord God, help me today to . . .

Day 64
The Tenth Step to Serenity

Continued to take personal inventory and when we were wrong promptly admitted it.

—The Tenth Step

Search me, O God, and know my heart; test me and know my anxious thoughts. See if there is any offensive way in me, and lead me in the way everlasting.

—Psalm 139:23, 24

The Lord's Prayer teaches me to ask for daily bread, and it also reminds me to seek forgiveness and forgive others daily. Just as the Bible teaches me to deal with my anger before the sun sets, I am learning to review my attitudes, actions, thoughts and words each day.

Working the Tenth Step faithfully teaches me to be concerned about only one day at a time. Facing my defects and weaknesses squarely on a daily basis insures my continuing sanity, serenity, and spiritual growth.

As I take this Step, I need to read the Scriptures and pray for God to reveal any defects of character or wrongs that I have overlooked, or have not discovered since taking the Fifth Step. Through such prayer and meditation on God's Word, I will develop a tender conscience and be open to the leading of God's Spirit on a daily basis. Then, I will avoid having a wrong spirit or attitude when I admit a wrong, or more quickly confess any wrongs I commit with true humility. Working the Tenth Step will help me eliminate destructive habits, and thus speed along my recovery.

Taking The Twelve Steps Journey as a believer in Jesus will help me evaluate myself according to valid, objective, God-given standards. If my ethical standards differ from God's and shift with the changing times or attitudes of others, then I will be tempted to justify behaviors that destroy others and myself. God spoke in the Scriptures to help me and others solve that problem.

To get the most from my spiritual awakening, I have decided to admit humbly and promptly any violations of God's moral law, the Law of Love. And I will pray for God to help me do all things from the pure motive of love for God and others.

As I grow closer to the Most Holy God, I will become more like God. And God will show me things I did not see when I took my Fifth Step. As He reveals these things to me, I will promptly admit these wrongs and pray for Him to help me do better. His Spirit will show me how to apply the Ten Commandments and the Law of Love in my everyday life.

I thank Jesus for dying in my behalf. I know that God will forgive me for all my wrongs as I practice the Prayer Steps to Serenity with a sincere and open heart.

Prayer for Today

God, grant me the Serenity to accept the things I cannot change, the Courage to change the things I can, and the Wisdom to know the difference. Lord God, help me today to . . .

Day 65
Reasons for Lack of Prayer

Continued to take personal inventory and when we were wrong promptly admitted it.

—The Tenth Step

Do not think of yourself more highly than you ought, but rather think of yourself with sober judgment, in accordance with the measure of faith God has given you.

—Romans 12:3

I must not consider my circumstances a good excuse for my lack of prayer. God's Word tells me to look in my heart for the real reasons I put myself and my use of time ahead of God's will for my life and spending time with God.

Way down and deep inside, perhaps I still sometimes feel hostility toward God and do not want to be with Him. Sometimes I still refuse to yield entirely to the Holy Spirit's leading. Sometimes I am still afraid to let go and let God take total control of my life. When I fail to follow God, before I realize it, my emotions have taken control over me.

I need to take a personal inventory each day and check for these indications that I may have been stepping backwards:

Have I been too hasty in my words and actions?

Has anger been arising unexpectedly within me?

Do I sense a lack of love for God and others?

Do I derive too much pleasure in eating and drinking?

Has my conscience been accusing me of misbehavior?

Have I been seeking my own will and honor?

Have I put too much confidence in my own power and wisdom?

I can trace the reasons for a lack of Quiet Time, prayer, and serenity to answering any of the questions above with a "Yes."

I am to live in the Spirit, but sometimes I refuse to walk in the Spirit. When this happens, my feelings become my lord and I become their slave. When I recognize any of the above symptoms, I must ask God to forgive me, free me from these defects, and once again fill me with His loving presence. By His grace, God will help me come to Him honestly, and He will give me the power to pray and joyfully seek His fellowship each day.

Prayer for Today

Dear God, help me to walk in faith and in the power of your Holy Spirit rather than follow my feelings. Whether I feel like praying or spending time with you or not, please help me to do so anyway and discover that this will give me serenity. Give me that joyful fellowship I really want and need with you all the day. Today, using the list above, I wait quietly for you to show me any weaknesses I still must overcome with your help. Today, please help me achieve the victory I seek through you, so I can overcome ...

The Tenth Step to Serenity

Day 66
Overcoming Satan

Continued to take personal inventory and when we were wrong promptly admitted it.

—The Tenth Step

For our struggle is not against flesh and blood, but against the rulers, against the authorities, against the powers of this dark world and against the spiritual forces of evil in the heavenly realms.

—Ephesians 6:12

I must never forget that Satan will always be my enemy. He wants to destroy my life, and he will use every weapon at his disposal. But thank God, through the weapon of prayer, Satan can be defeated. No wonder Satan will do his best to take this weapon from my hands or try to keep me from using it.

Satan will tempt me to postpone prayer or shorten my time in prayer. He will influence my thoughts to wander and bring distractions into my mind. Sometimes he can sway me toward unbelief and hopelessness. He can also influence me to give up working The Twelve Steps, quit the Program, or stop attending the meetings of my Fellowship.

Nevertheless, I can overcome Satan and return to happiness when I hold fast and keep using my weapon of prayer against all obstacles. When our Lord was in Gethsemane, as Satan attacked more viciously, He prayed more fervently. I can do the same. Jesus prayed, and did not cease until He rose victorious. I can follow His example, and His Spirit in me will help me win the battles I face daily.

Without daily prayer and self-examination, Satan can quickly gain a foothold in my life. I must pray; for without prayer, the helmet of salvation, the shield of faith and the sword of the Spirit (which is God's Word), will have no power to defend me and defeat my spiritual foes. As the Bible teaches, "Therefore put on the full armor of God, so that when the day of evil comes, you may be able to stand your ground, and after you have done everything, to stand. Stand firm then, with the belt of truth buckled around your waist, with the breastplate of righteousness in place, and with your feet fitted with the readiness that comes from the gospel of peace. In addition to all this, take up the shield of faith, with which you can extinguish all the flaming arrows of the evil one. Take the helmet of salvation and the sword of the Spirit, which is the word of God. And pray in the Spirit on all occasions with all kinds of prayers and requests. With this in mind, be alert and always keep on praying for all the saints" (Ephesians 6:13-18). All depends on God and His promises, and persevering prayer enables Him to fulfill these quickly. May God be gracious and teach me to believe in Him and the power of daily prayer.

Prayer for Today

Dear God, give me the power to persevere in prayer. Do not let Satan rob me of the serenity I have found in you. Help me to see clearly every enemy, so I can direct my prayers toward defeating them. Keep me from blaming others, if they bear no responsibility. Keep me from accusing myself, if I bear no blame. Do not let Satan deceive me, but let me see exactly what he is doing so I can use prayer wisely and according to your Word. Today, I ask that your Holy Spirit would move me to spend more time with you, and help me to turn more to you from . . .

Day 67
I Train with a Goal

Continued to take personal inventory and when we were wrong promptly admitted it.
—The Tenth Step

Everyone who competes in the games goes into strict training... Therefore I do not run like a man running aimlessly.
—1 Corinthians 9:26, 27

By walking in The Twelve Steps Journey, I am bringing order into my life. I am learning to work the Steps each day. Sometimes I have slipped back into old attitudes and behaviors, and have said and done things that have hurt others and myself. When this has happened, I have needed to promptly admit my wrongs and make amends where necessary; otherwise, the loss of my serenity has often led me to worse thoughts, words and actions. I have learned that sometimes I need to pray The Serenity Prayer several times a day; especially when I am tempted to succumb to my cravings or weaknesses.

I need to remember I am in strict training for a spiritual goal. I need to give up everything that might be attractive but harmful to my spiritual growth. Each day, when I take a new personal inventory, I need to ask myself what things I could have omitted or added that day as a part of my training.

Jesus wants me to have an undivided heart. He does not want me to strive for earthly prizes and glory as though these were more important than the upward call and the heavenly prize. Have I been spending more time preparing myself for earthly success and accolades than I have for the eternal rewards of righteousness?

The Apostle Paul would not let anything deter him from pressing toward the mark for the prize. No self-pleasing in eating and drinking; no comfort or ease kept him for a moment from showing the spirit of the cross in his daily life. No thought of putting himself first kept him from sacrificing his all for his Master. Likewise, the cross needs to be the goal of my life too.

O God, give me the spirit of the cross through the power of the Holy Spirit. When the death of Christ works in me, I will make His life known to others through me. Jesus humbled himself and became obedient unto death on the cross. O Jesus, give me this attitude and show me daily what I need to do in order to pick up my cross and follow you.

Prayer for Today

Dear God, help me evaluate my life in the light of the cross each day so I will never rest satisfied with my spiritual, material, physical or mental attainments. Help me avoid the temptation to prize serenity so highly that I become unwilling to suffer for you and your cause. Today, I admit to you that I am still having trouble and need your help with . . .

The Tenth Step to Serenity

Day 68
Abiding in Christ

Continued to take personal inventory and when we were wrong promptly admitted it.

—The Tenth Step

We always carry around in our body the death of Jesus, so that the life of Jesus may also be revealed in our body.

—2 Corinthians 4:10, 12

As I pray through these Steps and continue my recovery, I see new heights to reach. Things I never thought of as wrong before now seem horrible. As the Holy Spirit works within me, He shows me things to remove that are incompatible with His full presence in my life. But most importantly, He wants me to be Christ-centered instead of me-centered.

As I spend more time in prayer, I am learning the meaning of abiding in Christ. At first, this meant to me simply affirming His presence with me each day. Now, I am learning that it also means abiding in the crucified Christ. Once, I thought I only had to affirm once and for all, "I am crucified with Christ." Now, I see that I am to abide daily in the fellowship of His death by taking the form of a servant.

Jesus humbled himself and became obedient unto death—this mind of Christ needs to be the spirit that marks my daily life. However, I need to pray that as I become more and more like Christ in His death, that I do not continue to sustain or return to destructive co-dependent relationships. The Holy Spirit will give me wisdom as I pray for His daily light in applying the Scriptures.

Jesus calls me to bear about in my body His dying for others and me. I am to live for the welfare of others. As I suffer with Christ, the crucified Lord can work out His life through me to help others. Am I doing this each day? Am I willing to do this? Am I willing for my self-centeredness to die, so a new Christ-centeredness will live? Am I willing to live so others can see Jesus alive and doing His best in me?

Prayer for Today

Dear God, as I take a moral and spiritual inventory each day help me consider these higher states of spiritual life, and not just my wrong deeds done as though these had no relationship to my life and death in Christ Jesus. As I take inventory at the close of each day, show me whatever things I have done that have destroyed the serenity of others, as well as my own serenity. Today, if there is anything keeping me from knowing more of the fullness of Christ in me, show me now what I lack so I can turn from . . .

Day 69
I Died on Christ's Cross

Continued to take personal inventory and when we were wrong promptly admitted it.
—The Tenth Step

Christ himself bore our sins in his body on the tree, so that we might die to sins and live for righteousness; by his wounds you have been healed.
—1 Peter 2:24

If I do not keep my eyes on Jesus as I review my life each day, I can become discouraged and think there is no hope for me. The things I hate doing, I seem to do repeatedly. I do not know how God can forgive me unless I remember that Jesus bore my sins in His body on the cross. Eventually, as His power works in me, Jesus will also give me the victory I seek over my temptations, compulsions and dependencies

I will not be able to live a righteous life unless I know that I have died to sin. The Holy Spirit needs to make my death to sin in Christ such a reality that I know myself to be forever free from its power. In addition, I need to yield myself completely to God, asking Him to forgive me and make me an instrument of righteousness.

It has not been easy for me to understand or experience what it means to die to sin and live to righteousness, but dying with Christ on His cross remains the key to victory over sin and temptation. By God's grace through faith, I actually shared with Christ in His death. To understand this will require self-sacrifice and earnest prayer: it will cost me a whole-hearted surrender to God and His will: it will require abiding and unceasing fellowship with the crucified and risen Christ.

If these things have not been my heart's desire, am I willing to recognize these as shortcomings? Or do I prefer to live on the level of law and morality instead of stepping up to the heights of a new spirituality? Will I resolve to love God with all my heart? Will I choose to make the effort to love and serve my neighbors? Or will I be satisfied with a low view of daily living?

As I pray through these Steps, resolving to live in full obedience to God, the Holy Spirit will show me the secret of dying with Christ, of dying to selfishness to live fully in God.

Prayer for Today

Holy Spirit, burn into my heart the meaning of having died to sin with Christ on the cross. Set me forever free from its dominion. As I trust you daily, give me power over every temptation and keep sin from reigning over me for Jesus' sake. When I am tempted to sin, remind me that practicing sin will destroy the serenity we enjoy together. Today, help me to live a sacrificial life. Help me to give up to you ...

Day 70
The Tenth Step and the Serenity Prayer

Continued to take personal inventory and when we were wrong promptly admitted it.

—The Tenth Step

*God, grant me the serenity to accept the things I cannot change, the courage to change the things I can, **and the wisdom** to know the difference.*

—The Serenity Prayer

We have not stopped praying for you and asking God to fill you with the knowledge of his will through all spiritual wisdom and understanding. We pray this in order that you may live a life worthy of the Lord and may please him in every way: bearing fruit in every good work, growing in the knowledge of God, being strengthened with all power according to his glorious might so that you may have great endurance and patience, and joyfully giving thanks to the Father.

—Colossians 1:9-12

Though Socrates did not originate the Greek aphorism, "Know Thyself," he focused on this maxim in his philosophical discussions. Several in my Fellowship have shown me that true humility and wisdom can result from knowing myself as I truly am. Having completed the Fifth Step, I know more about myself, and have acknowledged more about myself, than when I entered the Program. I now see myself more clearly, as others probably saw me when I was at my worst. After completing the Ninth Step, I saw the kind of person I could become—one who walks with honesty, honor, and integrity. As God removed my character defects and I made amends to others, those closest to me began to thank God for the person I was becoming—one Prayer Step at a time. Because I know myself better, I know that I could never have completed this much of the Program apart from the grace of God and His answers to my prayers and the prayers of others.

In order to continue my spiritual growth and progress, make wise decisions, and maintain a good relationship with others insofar as that is possible, I need to take personal inventory everyday. Some in my Fellowship pray to God when they first awake in the morning. They pray for God to help them overcome any remaining character defects throughout the day. They pray for God to give them the wisdom to do those things that will help them maintain their serenity that day—thus remaining open to God's grace when temptations come their way. Others in my Fellowship end the day with a Quiet Time and an evaluation of how their day went—confessing to God any wrongs they committed during the day. Then, they ask God for the wisdom and strength of character to make amends and seek the forgiveness of those they wronged.

The Tenth Step wisely directs me to promptly admit my wrongs. Praying and taking personal inventory throughout the day will help me avoid destructive situations and correct my errors immediately—when correction will be the easiest and most effective for others and me. The wisdom I receive from opening my heart to God's direction and protection moment by moment all the day long can help me see the way of escape when temptations come my way. God will give me the power to follow His guidance if I work the Tenth Step with prayer whenever needed throughout the day. I can pray The Serenity Prayer and ask God for the wisdom to live in such a way that my wrongs will be few. Each evening, my daily personal inventory can become a blessed time when my conscience commends me for my decisions, words, and actions.

Socrates encouraged us to know ourselves. The Bible also teaches us to know God and the will of God. Spiritual wisdom and practical understanding flow from knowing and following the will of God, which I learn from the Bible, the example of Jesus Christ, and the leading of the Holy Spirit—Who will always lead me in ways that are consistent with the Bible's commands and teachings.

God removes my character defects as I prayerfully focus on living in such a way that others can see the beauty and glory of Jesus Christ, Who lives in me. If I make it my goal to please Jesus Christ in every way, then when I am tempted to do wrong, I will follow Him and turn from all my temptations. If I ever fall into a temptation and do wrong, then I can go back to Him immediately, admit my wrong promptly to Him, ask Him to forgive me, and pray that He will give me the wisdom and strength to make right the wrongs I did.

As I practice the Prayer Steps to Serenity, God will remove my character defects, enable me to live in ways that are not characterized by wrong doing, give me the endurance to keep standing strong and resist temptation, help me remain patient in my afflictions and trials, and give me a joyful heart toward God.

Prayer for Today

Dear God, help me become more humble before you and others, so I can admit my wrongs promptly and begin to make things right immediately. Give me the wisdom to avoid situations and relationships that almost always lead me into wrong doing. Help me remember those times and recognize those situations when I will need to be the most prayerful and remember to pray The Serenity Prayer the most fervently. And now, I pray that you will give me the wisdom, the perseverance, and the courage to practice a daily Quiet Time and take a daily personal inventory each day at the special time of . . .

Prayer Step Principle

When people regard iniquity in their hearts, at the time of their prayers before God, it is as though a great impenetrable wall is separating them from God. "If I had cherished sin in my heart," said the psalmist, "the Lord would not have listened; but God has surely listened and heard my voice in prayer."

John Bunyan in *How to Pray in the Spirit*

The Twelve Steps Journey
Step 10 Workbook

Continued to take personal inventory and when we were wrong promptly admitted it.
—The Tenth Step

He who conceals his sins does not prosper, but whoever confesses and renounces them finds mercy.
—Proverbs 28:13

Things I have learned about God and prayer:

Things I have learned about myself:

What I have learned about a daily moral and spiritual inventory:

What I have learned about others and my relationship with them:

My prayer requests and answers to prayer:

Prayer for Today

God, grant me the Serenity to accept the things I cannot change, the Courage to change the things I can, and the Wisdom to know the difference. Lord God, help me today to . . .

Day 71
The Eleventh Step to Serenity

Sought through prayer and meditation to improve our conscious contact with God, praying only for knowledge of His will for us and power to carry that out.

—The Eleventh Step

For physical training is of some value, but godliness has value for all things, holding promise for both the present life and the life to come.
—1 Timothy 4:8

The Prayer Steps to Serenity help me contact God and understand Him for myself. The Twelve Steps Program of some recovery groups gives complete freedom of belief or unbelief, because they try not to be specifically religious. Their primary concern is recovery from addictions, compulsions, codependent relationships, emotional disorders, weaknesses, and others shortcomings in this life. Many such groups serve a valuable role in helping people overcome their problems and weaknesses in this life. The Prayer Steps to Serenity help me discover and maintain an eternal perspective that will bless me forever.

Since many philosophies and religions teach different and often contradictory things about God and eternity, they cannot all be teaching what is real and true about God. Having come this far in my recovery, and having a clearer head and purer intentions, I now have the opportunity to discover more about the true God as I work Step Eleven and bow before God in prayer and humility.

The Christian faith throughout the ages has taught some things from the Bible that almost every church and denomination proclaim as of central importance. By using the Bible as my standard and thinking about what the Church has taught for centuries, I can come to accept some bedrock truths that will help me now and forever. As I study the Bible, Christian literature, and listen to other Christians, God will teach me more about himself. If I seek the knowledge of God's will only and the power to carry it out, then He will teach me more about himself each day and show me how to discern truth from error.

I have discovered that Christian meditation will differ from the Eastern way. The Bible teaches me to meditate on its teachings. And it shows me how to apply them. The Scriptures teach God's way and will for everyone. For example, I can meditate on the Lord's Prayer by thinking about ways I can "hallow," honor, show respect for, and teach others about God's Name. Or, I can thank God for all the names He applied to himself in the Bible so I could know a lot more about Him; names such as, "The Lord will provide" and "Savior."

Christian meditation will turn me from self-interest and self-direction to putting first things first—God and God's way for my life. Such meditation will also protect me from following powers and guides that will deceive and eventually destroy me. Through working the Eleventh Step, I have found out by experience that my recovery goes better when I seek first the will of God and His power for my life.

Prayer for Today

God, grant me the Serenity to accept the things I cannot change, the Courage to change the things I can, and the Wisdom to know the difference. Lord God, help me today to...

The Eleventh Step to Serenity

Day 72
True Prayer Leads to True Fellowship

Sought through prayer and meditation to improve our conscious contact with God, praying only for knowledge of His will for us and power to carry that out.

—The Eleventh Step

To them God has chosen to make known among the Gentiles the glorious riches of this mystery, which is Christ in you, the hope of glory.

—Colossians 1:27

True prayer gives me contact with God. As I seek the holiness of God by persistent prayer, God removes my sinfulness with His holiness. As I get to know God better, my understanding of His greatness and power makes me more humble and I know by experience that He cleanses me from all sin.

True prayer leads me to see that I can have fellowship with God only if I choose the road of humility, just as Christ humbled himself. When

Jesus becomes my daily example and guide in prayer, I truly live in Christ, just as Christ lives in the Father.

Above everything, true prayer consists in fellowship with God, with God's bringing me under the power of His holiness and love. Through daily contact with God, He possesses me and stamps my entire personality with the lowliness of His Son. In friendship with my Redeemer, I find the secret of true love.

In Jesus Christ, I draw near to God. I have died with Christ, so Christ can reign in my life. By the power of the Holy Spirit, I need to affirm with assurance, "Christ lives in me."

Praying to the Father in the name of Jesus causes me to experience new joys and gives me greater power in prayer. I pray that God will strengthen me, and encourage me to believe in the certain victory He will bring. Trust in Him will give me the daily serenity I seek. Through true prayer, I can receive blessings that are greater than I could imagine. God will do this for all who love Him, so I pray for Him to keep my love constant and sincere.

I have found that daily victory in prayer does not come immediately or all at one time. God's fatherly patience continues toward me: He bears with His children. I rejoice in the promises I find in God's Word. In addition, as my faith grows stronger through prayer, I will persevere to the end and enjoy victory over my self-centeredness and selfishness.

Prayer for Today

Dear Jesus, I feel my spirit thriving through daily prayer, make me ever more willing to be humble or be humbled, so I can always enjoy sweet communion and serenity with you. Today, I seek . . .

The Eleventh Step to Serenity

Day 73
God Will Not Forsake Me

Sought through prayer and meditation to improve our conscious contact with God, praying only for knowledge of His will for us and power to carry that out.

—The Eleventh Step

Those who know your name will trust in you, for you, LORD, have never forsaken those who seek you.

—Psalm 9:10

When I pray for more of the Holy Spirit to help me in my weakness and draw me closer to God, I need to remember that the Holy Spirit wants more of me too. The Spirit of God wants to possess me entirely. Just as my soul indwells my body, so my body can serve me, the Holy Spirit wants to indwell my body and soul fully, so I can serve God. God wants His dwelling entirely under His control.

Until I have learned to trust God fully, I will not be ready for this new

Step. As God demonstrates His love and faithfulness to me daily, He will overcome my fear of giving Him such total control of my life. Such total commitment will result naturally, if I go to God in prayer and surrender each day to His care.

As I work through The Twelve Steps with reliance on God, the Holy Spirit will gently lead me to make entirely new and deeper consecrations to God. The Spirit will inspire me to seek more and more of God in my personal experience. The Holy Spirit will show me how Jesus Christ will deliver me from all my character defects and never forsake me. Jesus Christ, the Almighty Deliverer, comes near to defend me and draw me nearer to God. The Holy Spirit will lead me in my prayers for deliverance until I find the victory.

The Spirit of God will help me forget myself and seek more of God in prayer. Eventually, He will make me willing to put my needs aside, so He can train me to intercede for others, especially those who need deliverance from the same afflictions I have suffered. The Holy Spirit will make me willing to trust God to carry out His plans for my life and His plans for those I love and care for.

Prayer for Today

Oh God, draw near. Help me to know the Holy Spirit more fully and the serenity of His presence. Make me conscious of the work you want to do in me, for others and me. Today, as I think of what is still keeping me from being filled with your Spirit, remove from my life . . .

Day 74
I Am Crucified to Overcome

Sought through prayer and meditation to improve our conscious contact with God, praying only for knowledge of His will for us and power to carry that out.

—The Eleventh Step

I have been crucified with Christ and I no longer live, but Christ lives in me. The life I live in the body, I live by faith in the Son of God, who loved me and gave himself for me.

—Galatians 2:20

As I have tried to work The Twelve Steps in the light of the Scriptures, I have found the lesson of the cross the most difficult to learn. Can I truly live sacrificially?

Jesus said, "Take my yoke upon you and learn from me, for I am gentle and humble in heart, and you will find rest for your souls. For my yoke is easy and my burden is light" (Matthew 11:29, 30). Through the love of

Christ on the cross, I am drawn to Him, and I receive His promise to help me bear my cross with perfect serenity each day.

Love makes everything easy: His love for me and my love for Him. I need to meditate day and night on His love for me as He died on the cross, until the Holy Spirit gives me personal assurance of His love and daily help in all my struggles.

I need the Holy Spirit to breathe into my heart daily "you are a child of God" and give me joy unspeakable. When I remember that the blood of Jesus washed away my sins, I have proof that God will never reject me—His child. Through the power of Jesus' shed blood, I am well-pleasing to God.

As I seek to know God's will daily, asking Him for the power I need to carry it out, I also need to see myself as a ruler and intercessor (a king and priest) in Jesus' name and for His sake. God will strengthen me through His power, so I can conquer my character defects, overcome my temptations, and be filled with courage and joy. He can enable me to care more about others and find ways to bring them true happiness.

God will also encourage me to intercede for others each day as I seek His will for my life that day. Through my prayers, others will more easily discover God's will for them.

Prayer for Today

Dear Jesus, I will not learn in Twelve Steps over a few months time what you have taught others after years of diligent, prayerful, study. Teach me more as I reach up to learn from your Word; and as you teach me, give me that serenity that passes all understanding because it comes from you. Today, I pray not only for myself, but I truly want to pray for your blessing to be upon . . .

The Eleventh Step to Serenity

Day 75
Reasons for Effective Prayer

Sought through prayer and meditation to improve our conscious contact with God, praying only for knowledge of His will for us and power to carry that out.

—The Eleventh Step

Therefore, confess your sins to each other and pray for each other so that you may be healed. The prayer of a righteous man is powerful and effective.

—James 5:16

Prayer avails much with God, and the history of His people proves it. Prayer is the one great power I can exercise to secure the working of God's almighty power in my life and the world.

The prayer of a righteous person avails much. The Scriptures mean the person whose righteousness is in Christ: not simply as a garment covering the person, but as an indwelling life-power in a person made new by Christ.

As I seek God, God's will for my life, and God's power to obey day by day, I will be what the Scriptures call "an instrument of righteousness" (Romans 6:13). My true joy and effectiveness in prayer will depend on my relying daily on the righteousness of Christ working in me. As I surrender to God, I will be more useful each day.

On the night before He died, Jesus gave His wonderful prayer promises to those who obey. "If you love me, you will obey what I command. And I will ask the Father, and he will give you another Counselor to be with you forever—the Spirit of truth" (John 14:15-17). "If you remain in me and my words remain in you, ask whatever you wish, and it will be given you ... If you obey my commands, you will remain in my love, just as I have obeyed my Father's commands and remain in his love" (John 15:7, 10). In so many words, Jesus promised that if I practice the Eleventh Step in His name, my prayers would be effective.

Only when a righteous person rouses his whole being to take hold of God will prayer avail much. The effective, fervent prayers of righteous people effect great things.

Wherever two or three righteous people agree, Jesus has promised to answer prayers in His name. I need to meditate on how much could be done if hundreds of the truly righteous in Christ united in prayer. How many could be helped both inside and outside my Fellowship if we united in prayer before, during or after each meeting?

As I continue to take The Twelve Steps Journey, may I see the importance of how I live my life in Christ before and after I pray in Christ. If my prayers are not effective, maybe I need to go back and work through some of the earlier Steps once again.

Prayer for Today

Dear Lord, help me each day to live up to all the truth I am learning, so I can claim your promises in my prayers and step out with serenity in my heart. Today, show me what I lack to be a righteous person, so I can prevail in prayer for others, and help me remove ...

Day 76
Reasons for Daily Prayer

Sought through prayer and meditation to improve our conscious contact with God, praying only for knowledge of His will for us and power to carry that out.

—The Eleventh Step

Give us each day our daily bread.

—Luke 11:3

Once, I was afraid to pledge that I would pray to God each day. I thought such a demand and commitment was altogether beyond me. And then, I discovered that I did pray each day for daily bread. Each day I did trust in God to help me in some ways at least.

Surely, if I have once yielded my whole heart to God's love and service, I should count it a privilege to take advantage of God's invitation to come into His presence with my every need and the great needs of others each day.

Do I still desire to live wholly for God? Jesus Christ gave himself for me, and His love now watches over me and works in me daily without ceasing. Surely, I will welcome the opportunity the Eleventh Step gives me to prove day by day that I am devoting my heart's strength to the interests of God's kingdom. Surely, I will rejoice in the honor of being asked to bring down God's blessings through daily prayer and meditation.

The Eleventh Step reminds me to call out to God each day for His power. My needs and the needs of others are far beyond my ability to meet without the promise of God's power. As I praise God for what His power has done for me and others in my Fellowship, I am amazed at what He has enabled us to carry out.

I need to pray for God to lead others of like mind to me, so we can pray and work together to accomplish His will. I have found great freedom and wonderful healing as I have taken this journey with others who have problems similar to mine. I will find great power, and be more effective in prayer, as God unites me with those who know Him as I do through Jesus. Surely, this must be an important part of my seeking God's will for my life.

Prayer for Today

Dear Jesus, help all those who still hesitate to work this Step with a total commitment. Help them to see the difference such a commitment has made in the lives of others, and the serenity that this commitment can give them. Help me to find others I can unite with in prayer to promote your purposes and your redeeming love. Today, as I pray for some one or some group that I can pray with on a regular basis, bring to my mind the names of those you have chosen for me, and today I will begin to pray for . . .

Day 77
The Eleventh Step and the Serenity Prayer

Sought through prayer and meditation to improve our conscious contact with God, praying only for knowledge of His will for us and power to carry that out.
—The Eleventh Step

*God, grant me the serenity to accept the things I cannot change, the courage to change the things I can, and the wisdom **to know** the difference.*
—The Serenity Prayer

All the angels were standing around the throne and around the elders and the four living creatures. They fell down on their faces before the throne and worshiped God, saying: "Amen! Praise and glory and wisdom and thanks and honor and power and strength be to our God for ever and ever. Amen!"
—Revelation 7:11, 12

Now I see more clearly how every meditation in *Prayer Steps to Serenity* intentionally applies Step Eleven. The true power in the Program comes from my conscious contact with God—an awareness that God is walking with me and holding the light to show the way. Every Step in The Twelve Steps Journey improves my conscious contact with God and opens my heart more wisely to receive His loving truth and influence. When I pray The Serenity Prayer on the Eleventh Step, God helps me know Him better, the difference knowing God makes, and the difference His wisdom makes over merely human opinions.

As I practice the Prayer Steps up to the limits of my understanding, I grow spiritually and God substantially heals me in undreamed of ways. After taking the time to reflect on the meaning and value of each Prayer Step, I know that for the last several weeks in my journey I have been praying very consciously every day for the knowledge of God's will and the power to carry it out. I know He has graciously heard my prayers. He knows my need of Him and His powerful guidance, so His Spirit encourages me to pray. I can know His purposes and the difference His power makes when I seek to do His will in everything, so I want to practice Step Eleven everyday.

In my Fellowship, we remind each other *First Things First*. I need to start each day with prayer *and* meditation, and not just prayer. To know more about God and His will for me, I need to spend time quietly meditating on God's Word, the Bible. Those who seem to work the Program with the greatest serenity and success have learned the secret of maintaining a daily Quiet Time. The Prayer Steps help me more when I quiet my mind, read the Step and the Scriptures, and then pause a few minutes and focus on their meaning for me. Only after reflecting on what the Step and the Scriptures mean to me do I then read and contemplate the meditation for the day.

My Serenity Group also gets more from the Prayer Steps when we first quietly focus on and think about the Step and the Scriptures. After our group Quiet Time, we discuss their meaning for us before reading, discussing, and applying the rest of the *Prayer Steps to Serenity* meditation. When we pray The Serenity Prayer at the start of our meetings, we consciously practice the Eleventh Step and come to know by experience the difference working the Program with God and each other can make in our lives and in our recovery.

The angels and the people gathered for worship around God's throne know God with an understanding far greater than mine. They know that God is worthy to receive my praise and thanks—not only for what God has done in my life and world, but also for God's holy, loving character. His character influences Him to bless me and meet my needs. I can learn more from the example of those who gather in heaven to worship God. From the Bible and my praying through the Program, I know that God has the wisdom, power, and strength to meet the needs of those who seek Him with all their heart. God's nature, loving character, and actions show that He is worthy of my worship and all the glory that I can attribute to Him for all that He has done and continues to do. I know that God deserves the humble adoration of every creature.

I can know God better when I take time each day to praise and worship God before I even begin to think about myself and my needs. By focusing first on worshiping God, I overcome my fears and find freedom from my addictions, compulsions, dependencies, and resentments. In worship, God fills me with joy, love, power, and serenity. Taking the time to honor God for the wisdom and strength He gives me throughout the day will help me improve my conscious contact with God and give me a more accurate knowledge of His will for me and the power to carry it out.

Prayer for Today

Dear God, you are truly dear to me and closest to my heart. You have done more for me through the Program than I deserve. You have done more for me through my Fellowship than I can ever repay. You have done more for me through my practicing the Prayer Steps than I ever imagined possible. Help me to always put you first at the beginning of each new day. Help me to humble myself before you and ask you to do with me whatever you will throughout the day. Today, I want to praise you first and foremost for . . .

Prayer Step Principle

It is the Holy Spirit who leads Christians to understand and apply the promises of Scripture. It is amazing that in no age have Christians fully applied the promises of Scripture to the events of life...because there has always be an amazing disposition to overlook the Scriptures as a source of light respecting the passing events of life.

Charles Finney in *Principles of Prayer*

The Twelve Steps Journey
Step 11 Workbook

Sought through prayer and meditation to improve our conscious contact with God, praying only for knowledge of His will for us and power to carry that out.

—The Eleventh Step

For to be sure, he was crucified in weakness, yet he lives by God's power. Likewise, we are weak in him, yet by God's power we will live with him to serve you.

—2 Corinthians 13:4

Things I have learned about God and prayer:

Things I have learned about myself:

What I have learned about maintaining a relationship with God:

What I have learned about others and my relationship with them:

My prayer requests and answers to prayer:

Prayer for Today

God, grant me the Serenity to accept the things I cannot change, the Courage to change the things I can, and the Wisdom to know the difference. Lord God, help me today to . . .

Day 78
The Twelfth Step to Serenity

Having had a spiritual awakening as the result of these Steps, we tried to carry this message to others, and to practice these principles in all our affairs.

—The Twelfth Step

Jesus said to them, "Go into all the world and preach the good news to all creation"

—Mark 16:15

Whenever a newcomer shows up at one of my meetings, I need to pray that God will help me welcome him or her in the right spirit and with the right words. With an open heart and mind, I will need to welcome them in such a way that they will be able to see what The Twelve Steps Journey has done for me. With the help of God, I will be able to encourage them by sharing what The Twelve Steps promise, and how God has helped me apply and live by the Steps I have taken and millions of others have taken in recovery.

Through prayer and meditation, God will show me when I am ready to share The Twelve Steps Journey and the Prayer Steps to Serenity with outsiders. Having experienced a spiritual awakening, I will have true spiritual substance and not theory to share with those who need to begin walking this walk of joy and inner peace. If I begin to teach others about The Twelve Steps without praying for God to lead me and guide me as I speak, this may actually hinder my recovery or delay someone else from entering into a recovery group or Fellowship.

Perhaps the best evidence for others that The Twelve Steps Journey works will be my practice of the Steps in all my affairs. Having recovered substantially from my addictions, compulsions, obsessions, depressions, co-dependencies, weaknesses, cravings, and fears, I can now walk in The Twelve Steps in all of my relationships as I need each Step. I can quit trying to control my wife or husband, my parents or children, my boss or my employees. I can release them to the care of God. I can admit that I am powerless to rule their lives, and I do not need to take their daily moral inventory to make myself feel better. I can let go and let God direct all my affairs and relationships, and give me the power to work the right Step whenever needed.

As I pray daily and meditate on the Word of God, I will grow spiritually, increase my knowledge of God, and be able to tell others more about Him and how He saved me from my sins and weaknesses. If others see I am not like the hypocritical so-called "believers" they have known, perhaps God will get the glory for my recovery and they will be open to receive God's help in their lives too.

Prayer for Today

God, grant me the Serenity to accept the things I cannot change, the Courage to change the things I can, and the Wisdom to know the difference. Lord God, help me today to . . .

The Twelfth Step to Serenity

Day 79
The Power of Intercession

Having had a spiritual awakening as the result of these Steps, we tried to carry this message to others, and to practice these principles in all our affairs.

—The Twelfth Step

We are therefore Christ's ambassadors, as though God were making his appeal through us. We implore you on Christ's behalf: Be reconciled to God.
—2 Corinthians 5:20

Let me consecrate myself to interceding more for others, and especially for those who need to work the Program. The Apostle Paul wrote of praying for those he had not even met. Though he was personally subject to the limitations of time and space, just as we are finite, in the Spirit he had power in the name of Jesus Christ to pray for a blessing on those who had not yet heard of the Savior, and so do we.

Let me pray each day for those who need to find God and deliverance, whether I know them personally or not. I can pray for the opportunity to tell them about God and the Journey that will free them from their bondage to destructive thinking and injurious actions. I can pray for God to give me just the right words to share with every needy person He brings across my path, whether inside or outside my Fellowship meetings.

Paul lived a heavenly life of love and amazing power in prayer, and so can I. If I start living a life of prayer, God will give me this same power. I need to pray for greater boldness and daring to reach up to heaven in the mighty name of Jesus Christ in order to bring down a blessing on those who need God, that they might be freed from despair, discouragement, fear, pride or other problems.

Imagine what would happen if more of those who walk in the Journey, say twice as many as before, could be brought by God's grace to pray for others with twofold faith and joy. A gentle power would come down in our Fellowship groups, if people would spend more time in prayer before and during our times together. Each one would experience and share the serenity we enjoy. If I prayed more (privately and with others), it would make a wonderful difference in the numbers of people I could help.

Prayer for Today

Dear Lord, help me to be more concerned about others, now that my life has changed so much and your serenity keeps me daily. Help me to keep working the Steps that I need, and lead me to others who need the type of help that I have been prepared to give through the Prayer Steps to Serenity you have taught me. Today, show me the groups or people that I need to become more involved with so I can share The Twelve Steps Journey with others...

Day 80
God Calls Me to Tell Others

Having had a spiritual awakening as the result of these Steps, we tried to carry this message to others, and to practice these principles in all our affairs.

—The Twelfth Step

But you will receive power when the Holy Spirit comes on you; and you will be my witnesses in Jerusalem, and in all Judea and Samaria, and to the ends of the earth.

—Acts 1:8

Since I have worked through The Twelve Steps Journey and have come to know my Savior more personally through prayer and obedience, I am now ready to point others to the Person and Program that can work for them.

Jesus called His servants to witness for Him, to testify to His wonderful love and power to redeem, to tell others about His continual abiding presence and wonderful ability to work miracles in their lives. Indeed, my spiritual awakening and recovery one day at a time qualifies as a miracle, especially when I look back and see what God has done through prayer. To witness, I simply need to tell what God and these Steps have done for me personally.

Witnessing is one of the most powerful weapons that God enables us to use in helping others experience the spiritual transformation we enjoy. Without claiming special authority or power, without worldly wisdom or eloquent speech, without social status or privilege, I need to witness by my life and actions. I can be a living proof and witness of what Jesus can do. In this way, I do not point with pride to myself, but humbly to Jesus as my Higher Power.

Not by my words only, but by my transformed life, the Spirit will bring others to the feet of Jesus for salvation here and hereafter. When the Holy Spirit filled the first disciples, they began to speak of the mighty things Jesus had done. I need to pray for the same Spirit to help others find the open secret that I have discovered through my spiritual awakening.

In the power of the Spirit, the disciples helped others in the name of Jesus. Filled with the life and love of Jesus, they spoke of what Jesus had done for them, and this gave the good news power to help others. Here we have the secret of a flourishing spiritual fellowship: every believer bearing witness for Jesus and telling what He does for people.

Prayer for Today

Lord Jesus, please give me the strength, serenity, courage, and humility to be a transparent witness in helping others, just like your first disciples led people to saving faith in you as Savior. Today, help me find one of my highest joys in telling others about you, your love and grace, and the Prayer Steps to Serenity that have set me free; show me . . .

Day 81
What May Set Me Apart

Having had a spiritual awakening as the result of these Steps, we tried to carry this message to others, and to practice these principles in all our affairs.

—The Twelfth Step

When the Counselor comes, whom I will send to you from the Father, the Spirit of truth who goes out from the Father, he will testify about me. And you also must testify, for you have been with me from the beginning.

—John 15:26, 27

Some have found help and sanity from sources other than The Twelve Steps Journey I have taken. Some view their higher power differently from me. I have learned not to proudly separate myself from them, or look down upon them, but thank God for them, and praise God for what He is doing in their lives thus far. God promised that those who seek Him with all their hearts will find Him. I pray for them to seek and find, to know and follow, to love and obey God more fully in Jesus Christ according to the Scriptures.

In working the Twelfth Step, I will tell others about what God and the Steps have done for me, and then let go and let God go to work. My prayers for courage to speak will help me, but my prayers for those I tell about God and the Steps will help even more—I can pray for others when I cannot be with them, and the Holy Spirit can touch their hearts and minds with the truth.

What may separate me from others in my Fellowship is the great truth that the Lord Jesus Christ saved me and helped me in my recovery. I will be saying that my spiritual awakening involved a new relationship with Jesus Christ. My telling about The Twelve Steps Journey will be similar to the first disciples: they ceased not in every house to teach and to preach Jesus Christ. My Higher Power is Jesus Christ, and I am not ashamed to say so, even though my loyalty to Him may set me apart from others. If this happens, I will pray that others see the sweet Spirit of Jesus in me and not the condemning arrogance or judgmental attitude they have sometimes seen in others.

God cleansed me to serve Him and others. Through The Twelve Steps Journey, when I was powerless, God restored me to sanity. Today, I find my life is creative, joyful, peaceful and full of God's love, and I have an everlasting hope that I will see the Lord of glory and spend eternity with Him and those who love Him. God taught me how to pray, and gave me His Spirit to teach me the Scriptures. God gave me a spiritual Fellowship and a message to share. I have much, and even more than I can say, for which to thank God.

Prayer for Today

Lord Jesus, thank you for saving me and restoring my sanity and serenity. Give me the courage to tell the full truth about you, my recovery, and the work of your Spirit in my life. May others come to know that they can have what I and many others have found in you. Today, by your grace, help me to overcome my fear of helping . . .

Day 82
My Personal Testimony

Having had a spiritual awakening as the result of these Steps, we tried to carry this message to others, and to practice these principles in all our affairs.

—The Twelfth Step

After they prayed, the place where they were meeting was shaken. And they were all filled with the Holy Spirit and spoke the word of God boldly. All the believers were one in heart and mind. No one claimed that any of his possessions was his own, but they shared everything they had.

—Acts 4:31, 32

I must base what I share with others about my recovery and serenity on my personal experience with God, prayer, the Scriptures, and The Twelve Steps Journey I am taking. I can show others the Jesus of the Bible, but showing them Jesus in my life may be more effective at first. By the grace of God, my recovery and restoration to sanity, one day at a time, will show what Jesus can do and not what I have done. Above all, I need to stay personal and demonstrate my love for them. Those who need to take the Journey have heard enough theories. They need to see what works and the One who works actually working in the lives of others.

The Holy Spirit will show what Jesus and following in His Steps can do as people look into my heart and see my life. If I rely on Jesus and ask Him to live His life daily through me, they may see the loving work of God in my life. I need to pray for the Holy Spirit to build me up, so I can walk in such fellowship with Jesus Christ that He can reveal himself through me. Only the Holy Spirit can lead me, and others, to understand the indispensable secrets of spiritual health and character development. One secret is a life of prayer and daily fellowship with God. Another secret is a childlike love for God and true consecration to the Father and the Son. And yet another secret is sharing the good news about God and His Program with others: working the Twelfth Step.

I cannot fake a true spiritual awakening and recovery, for others will see through me to the discredit of Jesus, The Twelve Steps Journey, and me. I cannot allow myself to fall back into kidding myself by faking some spiritual trip. I need to pray that the spiritual truths I read about or discover (which I do not fully understand yet), will still be revealed to me personally by the Holy Spirit in some small way each day—for Christ's sake, for my sake, and for the sake of others.

Prayer for Today

Dear Father, unite me with others of like heart and mind, those who know you personally and the power of your Holy Spirit in working The Twelve Steps. Teach us to pray together, that your power might spiritually awaken other needy souls and show them the path to serenity. As I think of what is still keeping me from showing forth Christ in my life, please . . .

Day 83
My Future Work: Carrying the Message

Having had a spiritual awakening as the result of these Steps, we tried to carry this message to others, and to practice these principles in all our affairs.

—The Twelfth Step

"Come, follow me," Jesus said, "and I will make you fishers of men."
—Matthew 4:9

The Lord Jesus now expects me to help others find fellowship with Him in recovery. Since I have found a Higher Power and Prayer Steps that work, since God's love now fills my heart and motivates me, I can carry the message to others more effectively. A part of my continuing recovery will depend on whether or not I remain God-centered and seek to share my testimony with others. I cannot allow myself to slip back into self-absorption and self-centeredness.

I have discovered the reason The Twelve Steps Journey works so well.

The Holy Spirit inspired some to see the pattern of Jesus' teachings and biblical practices in The Twelve Steps. The Twelfth Step teaches those in recovery what God's Word teaches everyone about their duty: the duty to pray for and help others.

When I keep my heart right with God, I have freedom in definite believing prayer and may expect God to bless my outreach to others. Having worked through The Twelve Steps, I understand the message so well that I can carry the message to others, but I need to remember to rely daily on God to prepare the way for others to learn about the Journey.

The health of my Fellowship and Serenity Group can be preserved only as those who benefit share the truths they are learning with others. The value of the Twelfth Step will be seen clearly when every member thinks about what could happen if each one worked this Step faithfully. Everywhere I look there are people who need help, and I cannot always expect someone else to do the work. As more of us join together in working Step Twelve, we can truly rejoice in a Serenity Celebration!

My success in carrying the message will depend upon my receiving more love for the Lord Jesus and more love for others. Working this Step consists in both speaking to others and speaking to God about others. I pray that I will always reach out to others with grace, love and mercy.

As I surrender my life to God's everlasting love, His love in me may bring many wanderers back to Him and give them healing. Someone reached out to me and led me to The Twelve Steps and the true God who inspired them. May I reach out to others so they will be able to overcome their weaknesses and find the joyful serenity they need.

Prayer for Today

Dear Father, keep me in everlasting fellowship and serenity with you. Enable me to help others find fellowship with you and life everlasting through faith in Jesus Christ. May others come to know through my life and words the power of the Holy Spirit to transform lives and restore broken relationships. Remind me of the Prayer Steps to Serenity that I may need to take each day. Now, I want to praise you and thank you for . . .

Day 84
The Twelfth Step and the Serenity Prayer

Having had a spiritual awakening as the result of these Steps, we tried to carry this message to others, and to practice these principles in all our affairs.
—The Twelfth Step

God, grant me the serenity to accept the things I cannot change, the courage to change the things I can, and the wisdom to know **the difference**.
—The Serenity Prayer

Praise be to the God and Father of our Lord Jesus Christ, who has blessed us in the heavenly realms with every spiritual blessing in Christ.
—Ephesians 1:3

I may not be able to make someone else's life better, but I can introduce them to the Prayer Steps and Program that can change and transform their life forever. No one needs to keep on living as I did before I found The Twelve Steps road to recovery and serenity. The Twelfth Step requires me to share the Program with others, and I know their walking in The Twelve Steps Journey can make an everlasting difference in their lives and in the lives of those they love.

Part of the power in the Prayer Steps rests in their universal application with God's help. No matter what problems my neighbors, friends, relatives, or even strangers face, I know that some of the solutions to their problems can be found in one or more of the Prayer Steps to Serenity. They may not be ready to work the whole Program, but I now know enough to share with them some of the time-tested truths that can make the difference in their lives.

Before I completed The Twelve Steps Journey, I had many hidden faults and character defects; some hidden not only from others but also hidden from myself. During my journey, I discovered that God had the power to remove these defects of character and bring wholeness back into my life, a wholeness that made the difference in all of my relationships. Almost everyone that I meet will be trying to hide something from others, and even from themselves. Knowing this universal human trait and the difference ridding ourselves of these defects can make, I know the value and importance of sharing the Prayer Steps message with others.

If I want to avoid new defects of character, I need to keep praying The Serenity Prayer; asking God to help me keep on applying the Prayer Steps principles in all I do. Committing myself to Twelfth Step work as I pray The Serenity Prayer daily will continue to make the difference in the way I live. If I start denying and hiding new defects of character, I will be robbed of my serenity and recovery. I need to keep practicing the principles I have learned in the Program for the rest of my life. As I grow, I will change everyday. Spiritual growth instead of spiritual decline depends on my actively practicing the Prayer Steps that restored my sanity and serenity. Remembering the difference that The Twelve Steps can make inspires me to keep pursuing the goals of the Program rather than settle back into a mind-numbing complacency, a false satisfaction that will influence me to forget about seeking God and His will for my life daily.

For my spiritual well-being and that of others in my Fellowship, I need to go to my group meetings regularly. However, my Fellowship and Support Group meeting must not exist just for myself and my friends. Working the Twelfth Step means I need to keep reaching out to others. I need to pray for those who need the help that I found to find my Fellowship, me, and the God who found us—so we can share with them the solutions we received from the Program. By giving away what God has given us through the Prayer Steps, we not only help others, we also help ourselves.

As I prepare to walk again through the Prayer Steps, I praise God for the difference He has made in me. God has blessed my walking in the path that He planned for me when He arranged for me to discover The Twelve Steps Journey. He brought the people and the Program into my life at just the right time, the time that I was most ready. His Spirit moved me in answer to many prayers—my prayers and the prayers of others—to begin working The Twelve Steps. I now know God more fully as my heavenly Father. I see how the Prayer Steps have drawn me closer to the Lord Jesus Christ. I know by experience the fullness of the Holy Spirit as He shares with me all the spiritual blessings made available to every believer in Jesus Christ. I pray that God will help me to always remember the difference that Jesus Christ has made in my life so I can be strong in His might and not fall back into compulsions and dependencies that will rob me of my serenity and sobriety.

Prayer for Today

Lord Jesus, you reign as the Lord of my life and Lord of the universe. You have shown me your love and the love of the Father for me. When I was hopeless, you gave me hope in you and you never failed to live up to my trust in you. Increase my faith in you and in your power to keep on working in my life as I live a life of prayer, praying as the Holy Spirit leads me and teaches me how to pray. Give me such a sense of your loving desire to help others that I will seek to share with them the truths that have saved me, for now and forever. Today, I trust in you and pray that you will help me share the spiritual blessing of knowing you and your saving grace with . . .

Prayer Step Principle

Be sober and humble. Go to the Father in the Name of His Son and tell Him your case. Go in the assistance of the Holy Spirit and with your understanding also in accordance with the Word of God.

John Bunyan in *How to Pray in the Spirit*

The Twelve Steps Journey
Step 12 Workbook

Having had a spiritual awakening as the result of these Steps, we tried to carry this message to others, and to practice these principles in all our affairs.

—The Twelfth Step

Carry each other's burdens, and in this way you will fulfill the law of Christ.

—Galatians 6:2

Things I have learned about God and prayer:

Things I have learned about myself:

What I have learned about the importance of sharing the Steps:

What I have learned about others and my relationship with them:

My prayer requests and answers to prayer:

Prayer for Today

God, grant me the Serenity to accept the things I cannot change, the Courage to change the things I can, and the Wisdom to know the difference. Lord God, help me today to . . .

Rejoicing in The Twelve Steps Journey

Rejoice in the Lord always. I will say it again: Rejoice! Let your gentleness be evident to all. The Lord is near. Do not be anxious about anything, but in everything, by prayer and petition, with thanksgiving, present your requests to God. And the peace of God, which transcends all understanding, will guard your hearts and your minds in Christ Jesus.

—Philippians 4:4-7

Rejoice! You have completed the first phase of your Twelve Steps Journey. You now have many Prayer Steps to Serenity in your heart and mind to guide you in the future. You now have time-tested tools to help you maintain your serenity in every situation or when faced with any problem. You can start every day with rejoicing, trusting that God is with you and for you and seeking to help you discover what is best for you and others. With His heart open to you, you know that God is only a prayer step away when you need help. Such assurance makes your heart glad in troubled times as well as good.

As you continue walking in the well-worn path of the book *Prayer Steps to Serenity*, you can rejoice in your Twelve Steps Journey every day.

You know that God lives in you as your Comforter, Counselor, Guide, and Power. You have available to you the prayer steps to God, who has the power to free you from any addiction, compulsion, or sin. You have access to God, who can give you the strength to endure with serenity any sickness or weakness that will not be healed in this life. God can heal any obsession or addiction substantially, so you can find joy and peace in your service to others. With God, you can face any obstacle with wisdom and courage. You can change some things with God's help, and maintain your serenity at all times.

As you practice daily The Twelve Steps Journey, you will draw closer and closer to the God of Love. As you continue to apply what you are learning in *Prayer Steps to Serenity,* you will find great joy in your relationships with others. You will find ways to share the love of God with everyone, and they will return the love of God to you. You can rejoice in your recovery—one day at a time.

When your spirit needs a lift, you now know where to find the Prayer Steps you need. When others need your help or encouragement, you now have access to the truths they need to hear. In addition, you can pray for guidance to share these truths in the right way and at the right time. You know good news about the path to recovery, and you have good news that you can share with those seeking that path. Through prayer, you can joyfully share the Good News with anyone. With God in you, you can share truths that change lives, and you can do so with God's infinite love pouring forth from you.

Now, while the Prayer Steps to Serenity are still fresh in your heart, pray for God to show you the next Step to take in your Twelve Steps Journey. Pray, "Lord, do You want me to begin a Serenity Group so I can share these prayer steps to recovery with others? What do You want me to do so I can find the support I need to maintain my serenity and recovery? Who is the first one in my Fellowship that I should talk to about these truths that mean so much to me? When should I speak to them? Prepare their heart and mind to hear and receive what I share with them. Show me what I am to do today. Amen." Then, wait for a nudging or word from the Spirit of God to begin showing you what to do first—one day at a time.

As you consider taking the Twelfth Step in your journey to serenity, pray, "Lord, is there one person that I should tell about this journey that

I am taking? Is there one person I should ask to go along with me? Lord, can you tell me now who that could be? If not, please show me in the coming days the person I need to reach out to help. Who is the new person that I need to speak to about the truths that I have learned about recovery and serenity? Amen." Now, wait and see if the Lord will give you a name, one or more names. This prayer may become the beginning of the support group you and others need—one person at a time.

After the Spirit has guided you in praying about your Twelfth Step, pray again, "Dear Father in heaven, prepare their mind and heart to receive what I hope to share with them. Please give me the right words to say, and move me to reach out to them according to your perfect timing. Show me when they are ready to listen, or draw them to me for the help I can give them on the road to serenity and recovery. Once we begin, help me to persevere to the end with the love in my heart that you have for them. Amen."

Pray before you take another Step. Pray for the Lord Jesus to help you find another person, prayer group, support group, Bible study group, Fellowship or church that will help you stay accountable to God, prayer, and walking the prayer steps to serenity in the power of the Holy Spirit. Pray before you close this book for today.

Prayer for Today

Dear God, show me what you want me to do next. How can I best serve you and others? You have given me many natural and spiritual gifts. Teach me how to use them so I can help others find you and the peace that only you can give. I rejoice in this journey. I praise you for what I have learned from the Bible, and I want to study your Word more faithfully. Thank you for leading me to take The Twelve Steps Journey, please show me now how I can share the good news of recovery and serenity with others as I pray specifically about . . .

Prayer Step Principle

Test the spirits by the Bible. People are sometimes led away by strange fantasies and sudden impulses. If you compare them faithfully with the Bible, you never need to be led astray. You can always know whether your feelings are produced by the Spirit's influences by comparing your desires with the spirit and tone of true faith as described in the Bible.

Charles Finney in *Principles of Prayer*

Creating Your Own Serenity Journal

The book *Prayer Steps to Serenity* contains generous white space for you to write your own meditations and thoughts. For example, consider adding your own reflections to each *Prayer Step Principle* page. The Twelve Steps Journey Workbook pages will also enable you to direct your thoughts and prayers through carefully phrased questions. You can answer these questions in your *Prayer Steps to Serenity* book, in the *Serenity Journal* that you create, or by using the special journals and pages available at PrayerSteps.org. For repetition, and to help you become accustomed to answering consistently essential questions, every question except the middle question in The Twelve Steps Journey Workbook is identical. The middle question relates directly to a central truth in that Step. Since there are seven daily devotional readings for each Prayer Step in this *New Serenity Prayer Edition*, you may need to take a longer or additional Quiet Time on the seventh day of each week to answer The Twelve Steps Journey Workbook questions for that Step.

Consider creating your *Serenity Journal* or *Recovery Journal* (for those working a different 12 Steps recovery program) in a separate notebook suitable also for group study. Use a loose leaf binder, so you can add more pages at the appropriate places each time you read through the book and discover new truths. Divide your Journal into twelve parts: one part for each of The Twelve Steps. Subdivide each of the twelve parts into your Group Journey Guides questions and your Twelve Steps Journey Workbook questions, so you can easily find your meditations and answers to particular Step questions. Consider adding a separate page for each of the daily devotions in *Prayer Steps to Serenity*, so you can write your reflections, prayers, prayer requests, and answers to prayer for each daily reading on these pages. Think about creating a calendar to chart your progress and easily record your answers to your prayers.

You may want to use your *Serenity Journal* and the questions in the Group Journey Guides and The Twelve Steps Journey Workbook in a small discussion forum, support group, or prayer group. Consider starting your own Prayer Steps Meeting, Prayer Support Group, Serenity Celebration, or Serenity Group (visit SerenityGroups.org for free materials and ideas). Encourage everyone to be sensitive toward those who are more reserved about discussing the confidential and intimate details of their lives or the thoughts they have written in their *Serenity Journal*. Focus your Prayer Steps Meeting, Serenity Group, or Serenity Celebration on helping each member grow spiritually, walk The Twelve Steps Journey, and find serenity.

Those who are the most honest with themselves will benefit the most from answering all the questions in The Twelve Steps Journey Workbook. By using the Group Journey Guides and The Twelve Steps Journey Workbook questions in a small group, you can help people be honest and receive the help they seek in their Program. You can create a lasting and valuable *Serenity Journal, Recovery Journal,* or *Prayer Steps Journal* by adding what you have learned in your support group. Do not record personal details shared by other members of your group, just insights into and applications of the *principles* you have studied and want to apply.

If we can serve you in other ways, visit us at PrayerSteps.org or SerenityGroups.org and complete the Contact E-mail Form. Please use the many free resources at PrayerSteps.org and SerenityGroups.org to help you and others continue in your journey and create different journals with the resource pages provided online. If you have additional ideas or have created additional resources to help others, please let us know at SerenityGroups.org or PrayerSteps.org.

Principles for Organizing Serenity Groups and Celebrations

Welcome everyone to your meeting. Encourage everyone to tell their first name (perhaps use name tags or name cards for tables). Open with a time of silence to focus people's attention on the purpose of the meeting. Offer an appropriate prayer, but if you call on someone to pray be certain they have agreed in advance to pray in the meeting. You might open simply with The Serenity Prayer and then close the meeting with The Lord's Prayer. Say something positive about your Serenity Group or Serenity Celebration and its purpose. Make people feel at home by telling them that no one needs to announce why they are there or talk about their weaknesses or problems, but that people are welcome to share their personal problems and weaknesses with your group.

Emphasize the importance of confidentiality. One tremendous value that comes from leading people in a Serenity Celebration or Serenity Group using *Prayer Steps to Serenity* is allowing people to maintain their privacy about their problems or weaknesses while they are learning about

The Twelve Steps Journey and the power of prayer to change people's lives. Some may come to your meetings who are involved in illegal and immoral activities. Your group can help them find the wisdom and serenity they will need to take their Fourth and Fifth Steps when they are ready. No one in your group will need to bear the burden of knowing someone is involved in illegal activity while they are seeking the help they need to change and become accountable for their actions. Remind people that your group is not designed to take the place of any other recovery program, Bible study, or prayer group. You simply want a group where people can talk openly and honestly about their Higher Power and the help God gives through prayer in our journey through life. You seek a group that can discuss the importance of faith, prayer, and the Bible, in the context of a 12 Steps Program.

Tell your group that *Prayer Steps to Serenity* will help everyone who takes The Twelve Steps Journey. Inform the group of which Step the meeting will focus on for prayer and serenity. Assure everyone that toward the end of the meeting you will give time to anyone who needs to ask a few brief questions about the other Steps in the Journey. Read one of the Prayer Step devotionals on the Step you plan to discuss. Perhaps supplement the reading with an appropriate reading from the Scriptures or from one of your other recovery books. Share an inspirational story, if appropriate. Begin answering the questions in the Group Journey Guides. Feel free to ask your own questions. Ask for additional questions or comments. Encourage discussion and respect personal privacy. Pray for anyone and his or her needs at any time during the meeting, for the Holy Spirit will not always prompt you to wait until the end of the meeting when the need is pressing.

By repetitive use of a consistent group-meeting plan, you will feel more comfortable and so will the new members or visitors that come to your meeting. Encourage newcomers to come back and stay with your group, no matter where you are in the group's Twelve Steps Journey. Assure them that you will repeat the journey and return to the Step they need. Tell them that everyone will be better prepared to discuss that Step, and share what they learned when taking that Step, after you have completed your current journey through all the Steps. Depending on your group's comfort level, you might make some time for people to pray quietly or aloud about what they need to take from the meeting to find the joy of recovery or maintain serenity.

At your Serenity Groups meetings, you might consider giving newcomers and members some of the free helpful handouts that you can copy, edit for your group, or print directly from this book's support web sites (available at SerenityGroups.org and PrayerSteps.org). You might also consider having some extra copies of *Prayer Steps to Serenity* at your meeting to give or sell to newcomers. Depending on their need and where they are in their recovery, some may prefer *Prayer Steps to Serenity The Twelve Steps Journey: New Serenity Prayer Edition* and others might need to begin with *Prayer Steps to Serenity: Daily Quiet Time Edition*. The *Daily Quiet Time Edition* is so inexpensive you might choose to give it freely to newcomers who cannot afford the book.

For a growing number of additional free personal and group resources, or to join an online Prayer Steps or Serenity Group, visit us often at PrayerSteps.org and SerenityGroups.org. If you have additional ideas to share or would like to announce the time and place of your Serenity Group or other prayer or support group meetings, please complete the Contact Form at SerenityGroups.org or write lgpjr@prayersteps.org and we will advertise your group through the web site.

Prayer Step Principle

Sudden temptations should not stop you from prayer and pouring out your soul to God; neither should your own heart's corruptions hinder you. Your business is to judge them and pray against them. Plead with God for grace and don't argue from discouragement and despair. David prayed this way: "For the sake of your name, O Lord, forgive my iniquity, though it be great."

John Bunyan in *How to Pray in the Spirit*

Group Journey Guides and Workbook

The Twelve Steps Journey Questions for Groups

Consider using or revising the questions below for each of your Serenity Groups meetings on each Step. The questions will be the same for each of the Steps in your Twelve Steps Journey. Consider making a different handout for each meeting on each of The Twelve Steps using these questions for each Step. Those in your Fellowship may want to put these handouts in their Serenity Journal. Additional free handouts for groups are available for editing or printing from the Serenity Groups web site at SerenityGroups.org.

Why do you think this Step may be hard for someone to take?

What do you think the greatest benefit from taking this Step will be?

How will taking this Step help others as well as the one taking the Step?

How will taking the Step get you further along on your journey?

Why do you think this Step will help someone find and maintain serenity?

How will prayer help someone taking this Step?

Do you wish to share any prayer requests or answers to prayer with the group?

What is the most important thing you learned in today's meeting?

What can you do to help more people work the Program or join your group?

What other questions or ideas would you like to discuss today?

The Twelve Steps of Alcoholics Anonymous

Step One

We admitted we were powerless over alcohol—that our lives had become unmanageable.

Step Two

Came to believe that a Power greater than ourselves could restore us to sanity.

Step Three

Made a decision to turn our will and our lives over to the care of God, as we understood Him.

Step Four

Made a searching and fearless moral inventory of ourselves.

Step Five

Admitted to God, to ourselves, and to another human being the exact nature of our wrongs.

Step Six

Were entirely ready to have God remove all these defects of character.

Step Seven

Humbly asked Him to remove our shortcomings.

Step Eight

Made a list of all persons we had harmed, and became willing to make amends to them all.

Step Nine

Made direct amends to such people wherever possible, except when to do so would injure them or others.

Step Ten

Continued to take personal inventory and when we were wrong, promptly admitted it.

Step Eleven

Sought through prayer and meditation to improve our conscious contact with God, as we understood Him, praying only for knowledge of His will for us and the power to carry that out.

Step Twelve

Having had a spiritual awakening as the result of these Steps, we tried to carry this message to alcoholics, and to practice these principles in all our affairs.

The Twelve Steps are reprinted and adapted with permission of Alcoholics Anonymous World Services, Inc. Permission to reprint and adapt The Twelve Steps does not mean that A.A. has reviewed or approved the content of this publication, nor that A.A. agrees with the views expressed herein. A.A. is a program of recovery from alcoholism—use of The Twelve Steps in connection with programs and activities which are patterned after A.A., but which address other problems, does not imply otherwise.

About the Author

L. G. Parkhurst, Jr. has been helping members of Alcoholics Anonymous and Al-Anon complete their Fifth Steps since 1975. As a pastor (to help and protect the anonymity of alcoholics, drug users, their family and friends), he started the first Al-Anon group to meet outside of the A.A. building in Rochester, Minnesota. His pioneering work led to the establishment of additional Al-Anon groups in other churches, resulting in a rapid growth of Al-Anon and other recovery programs.

He has a Master of Divinity degree from Princeton Theological Seminary, Princeton, New Jersey, and a Master of Arts degree in Philosophy and a Master of Library and Information Studies degree from the University of Oklahoma, Norman, Oklahoma. He serves as the pastor of Stonegate Cumberland Presbyterian Church in Edmond, Oklahoma. His church web site is StonegateChurch.org. Visitors are always warmly welcomed at Stonegate Church.

He is the author of *How God Teaches Us to Pray: Lessons from the Lives of Francis and Edith Schaeffer*, Word, UK, *Francis Schaeffer: the Man and*

His Message, Tyndale House Publishers, and *Francis and Edith Schaeffer*, Bethany House Publishers. He has compiled numerous devotional and prayer book classics; including, *How to Pray in the Spirit* from the writings of John Bunyan, Kregel Publications; *Answers to Prayer* and *Principles of Prayer* from the writings of Charles G. Finney, Bethany House Publishers; *The Believer's Secret of the Abiding Presence* from the writings of Andrew Murray and Brother Lawrence, and *The Believer's Secret of Intercession* from the writings of Andrew Murray and C. H. Spurgeon, Bethany House Publishers. Since 1989, he has written the weekly Bible Lesson for *The Oklahoman*, Oklahoma's oldest and largest daily newspaper. Most recently, he has compiled and edited Charles G. Finney's messages on Romans in *Principles of Righteousness: Finney's Lessons on Romans, Volume I*; to be followed by *Principles of Peace* and *Principles of Joy in the Holy Spirit*. These books are also published by Agion Press.

Recommended Reading

Answers to Prayer by Charles G. Finney. Compiled and Edited by L. G. Parkhurst, Jr. Published by Bethany House Publishers, Minneapolis, Minnesota, 1983, 2002. ISBN: 0-7642-2594-4

Learn the Secrets to Answered Prayer!

Charles Finney's amazing prayer life undergirded his forty-year preaching ministry. He often prayed for the conversion of entire towns. Here in his own words are the remarkable results of his prayers. This collection of answered prayers inspires and instructs all Christians who desire a deeper and more effective prayer life.

Each of the thirty devotional studies includes a principle from Finney's teaching on prayer, an excerpt from his autobiography, and a question for thought or discussion.

Charles G. Finney, widely acknowledged as one of America's foremost evangelists, was also a great man of prayer. God converted more than a half a million people through his ministry in the 1800's.

Principles of Prayer by Charles G. Finney. Compiled and Edited by L.G. Parkhurst, Jr. Published by Bethany House Publishers, Minneapolis, Minnesota, 1980, 2001. ISBN: 0-7642-2476-X

Learn How to Pray With Power!

Charles Finney's ministry rolled like a spiritual shock wave across the American landscape in the nineteenth century. He attributed his effectiveness in large part to prayer. Now his superb insights are condensed and collected in a single book.

Principles of Prayer provides a 40-day devotional study for those desiring to pray with power and see results. Each daily reading—through meditation, application, and prayer—will help you grow to Christian maturity.

How to Pray in the Spirit by John Bunyan. Compiled and Edited by L.G. Parkhurst, Jr. Published by Kregel Publications, Grand Rapids, Michigan, 1991, 1998. ISBN: 0-8254-2085-7

John Bunyan wrote, *"Pray often, for prayer is a shield to the soul, a sacrifice to God, and a scourge to Satan. Prayer will cease a man from sin; or sin will cease a man from prayer."*

John Bunyan was imprisoned in 1660 for "unlicensed" preaching in Bedford, England. Besides composing his classic work, *Pilgrim's Progress*, during twelve years of intermittent confinement, Bunyan also learned that the only way to glorify God in his sufferings was to pray often and pray devoutly. His thoughts and meditations on prayer were forged on the anvil of religious persecution, and it was from prison that he wrote, *True prayer is a sincere, sensible, affectionate pouring out of your heart and soul to God."*

How God Teaches Us to Pray: Lessons from the lives of Francis and Edith Schaeffer. Founders of L'Abri Fellowship. By L. G. Parkhurst, Jr. Published by Word Books, Nelson Word Ltd. Milton Keynes, England, 1993. ISBN: 0-85009-585-9   This publishing house has ceased to operate and the book is no longer in print. You can read the complete text for free online by visiting PrayerSteps.org.

Francis and Edith Schaeffer founded L'Abri Fellowship in Switzerland to demonstrate the reality of God through prayer.

Relying on prayer at every turn, they prayed for God to send provisions, plans and workers. God's answers to their prayers showed the manifest presence of God to those around them, especially unbelievers.

How God Teaches Us to Pray takes thirty-one examples of different types of answered prayer from their lives and works, and shows how any believer can pray, live and have as close a walk with God as the Schaeffers.

Principles of Righteousness: Finney's Lessons on Romans, Volume I. Complied and edited by L. G. Parkhurst, Jr. Published by Agion Press, Edmond, 2006. ISBN: 0-97780-530-1

Charles Finney founded and later became the President of Oberlin College. He is best known for his preaching and theology, which helped form the basis for The Twelve Steps of A.A. His messages on Romans are being collected in a three volume set; including the forthcoming *Principles of Peace* and *Principles of Joy in the Holy Spirit*. To learn more about the new Finney's Principles series, visit FinneysPrinciples.com.

Discover Your Needs	Remove Your Defects
Reach Beyond Yourself	Think of Others
Trust in God	Right Your Wrongs
Examine Your Life	Practice Doing Right
Admit Your Mistakes	Pray to God
Transform Your Thinking	Seek to Serve

As a gift, *The Daily Quiet Time Edition* of *Prayer Steps to Serenity* offers your family and friends a gentle, nonjudgmental, and non-threatening introduction to the 12 Steps. This abridged edition of *Prayer Steps to Serenity* includes sixty meditations that introduce those in denial, or those who do not want to work a 12 Steps Program, to the basic life-changing truths to be found in the 12 Steps. This edition includes sixty edited meditations from *Prayer Steps to Serenity* that can also be used in churches, home Bible studies, prayer groups, and other support groups.

Order the Prayer Steps Power Pack Today

Use this handy order form to order

Prayer Steps to Serenity The Twelve Steps Journey New Serenity Prayer Edition
&
Prayer Steps to Serenity Daily Quiet Time Edition

includes Free Shipping!

Enclose a check or money order to order the following books:

Prayer Steps to Serenity New Serenity Prayer Edition:	$18.95
Prayer Steps to Serenity Daily Quiet Time Edition:	$12.95
The Prayer Steps Power Pack (includes both books above):	$30.00

With Free Shipping, Please Ship My Books To:

Name: _____
Address:_____
Address:_____
City:_____ State:_____ Zip:_____

Please also autograph my books to:

Send your order and make your check payable to:
Agion Press, PO Box 1052, Edmond, OK 73083-1052
Order online at www.AgionPress.com

www.ingramcontent.com/pod-product-compliance
Lightning Source LLC
Chambersburg PA
CBHW031239290426
44109CB00012B/363